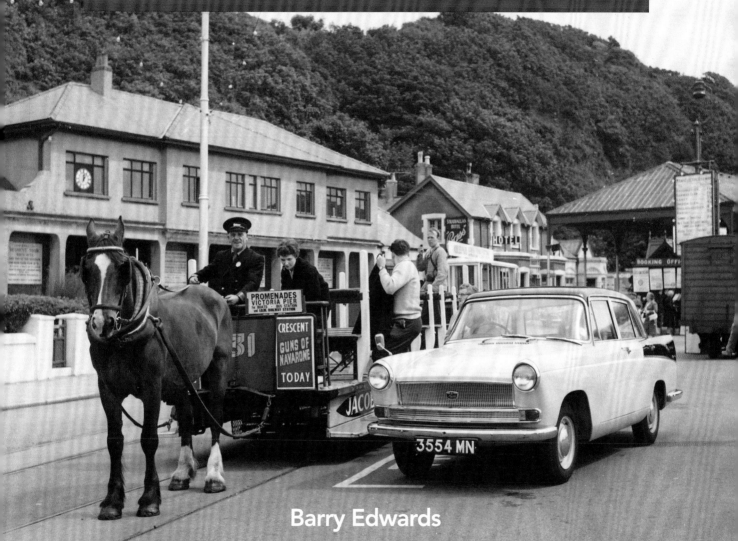

ONE HORSE POWER

Barry Edwards

The Douglas Bay Horse Tramway since 1876

Four retiring tram horses pose with Tramway stable staff in the small yard behind the terraced houses. The picture is dated August 1964. (MANX NATIONAL HERITAGE)

Lily
Publications

Dedication

This book is dedicated to the memory of my late mother, Monica Edwards. While discussing possible destinations for a family holiday in early 1976, Mum suggested the Isle of Man. The holiday was booked, by chance coinciding with the centenary of the Douglas Bay Horse Tramway.

CONTENTS

Double deck tram No. 14 on display in the Manx Museum in Douglas. The tram is surrounded by other transport exhibits and memorabilia. (AUTHOR)

Title page photograph: Farghers & Ashtons Ltd of Westmorland Road, Douglas, later Mylchreests Motors, used Horse Tram No. 31 as a back drop to photograph this newly registered 1500cc Austin A55 in May 1961. The vehicle was first registered on 20 May 1961 and described as a five seater in black and grey. Horse tram 31 was 67 years its senior having entered service in 1894. (MANX NATIONAL HERITAGE)

INTRODUCTION

The Douglas Bay Horse Tramway operates today on a 1.6 mile (2.57Km) 3ft (0.194m) gauge double track down the middle of the Douglas Bay Promenades from Derby Castle at the northern end to the Sea Terminal at the southern end. The line opened on 7 August 1876, just over 142 years ago, at a time when tourism on the Island was flourishing and the tramway went from strength to strength, being extended several times and with an ever increasing fleet of trams and horses.

Through two World Wars, financial crises, declining passenger numbers, and in more recent times, abandoned by Douglas Corporation, the tramway has emerged into Government ownership, with refurbished trams and a planned complete relay of the track, as part of the Douglas Promenade refurbishment, albeit with a single track and passing loops, from Esplanade Lane to the Sea Terminal. There will also be a new replica car shed on the existing site at Derby Castle, providing modern protection for the historic fleet of trams and the original stables have been secured for the future.

Perhaps most importantly, visitors and residents alike will be able to enjoy the delights of this unique Victorian tramway for many more years to come.

My sincere thanks go to all the management and Staff of Isle of Man Railways, Wendy Thirkettle and the team in the Manx National Heritage Library and Richard Kirkman for the excellent maps. Thanks also to Thurstan Denne, Cade Williamson and Jon Wornham for photographic material, and Deborah Watterson for her knowledge of the 'Trammers'; Ian Smith at Camrose Media, and Miles and Linda Cowsill at Lily Publications for the invitation and allowing me freedom in the content of this volume.

Barry Edwards
Ballasalla, Isle of Man,
October 2018

Opposite: Tram No. 36 is rushed past the impressive Villa Marina by an unidentified horse on 29 April 2018. (AUTHOR)

The Douglas Bay Horse Tramway

2018

- ◉ stops - Sea Terminal > Derby Castle
- ◉ stops - Derby Castle > Sea Terminal

Derby Castle
Depot

The Stables

Regency Hotel

Queens Promenade

The Hydro

Falcon Cliff Lift

Central Promenade

The Palace Hotel

Castle Mona Hotel

Castle Terrace

Broadway

The Esplanade

Villa Marina

Harris Promenade

Gaiety Theatre
The Sefton Hotel

Loch Promenade

Granville Street

Loch Promenade

Howard Street

Regent Street

Victoria Street

Clock Tower

Sea Terminal

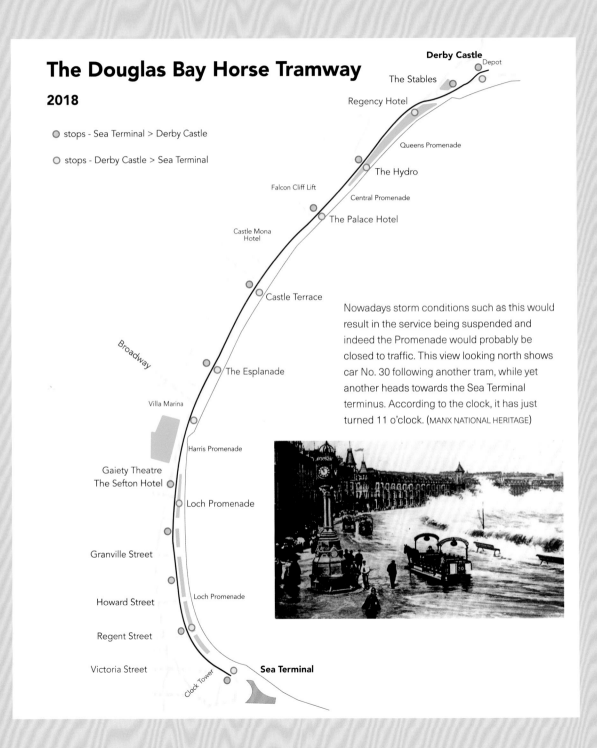

Nowadays storm conditions such as this would result in the service being suspended and indeed the Promenade would probably be closed to traffic. This view looking north shows car No. 30 following another tram, while yet another heads towards the Sea Terminal terminus. According to the clock, it has just turned 11 o'clock. (MANX NATIONAL HERITAGE)

A TRAMWAY IS BORN

In the early 1870s Douglas was a very different looking place than it is today. There was no Loch Promenade, and the houses and shops of Strand Street backed onto a somewhat uneven sea wall. From the end of Castle Street ran Colonel's Road to the north, and onwards to Castle Mona Road, all now Harris and Central Promenades. This area had been widened by 74ft into the sea in 1864, initially covered with lawns. Moving northwards there was the Villa

A fascinating view of the widening of the Promenade opposite Derby Castle terminus. The properties on Strathallan Crescent still exist and the three terraced houses in front of the stables are visible behind the crane in the centre of the picture taken on 28 January 1939. (MANX NATIONAL HERITAGE)

The Douglas Bay Horse Tramway

New configuration

Sea Terminal - Loch Promenade

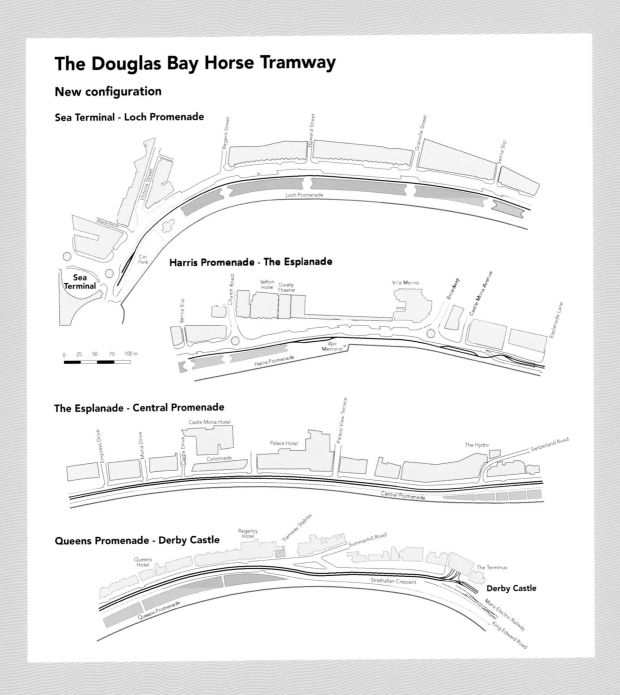

Harris Promenade - The Esplanade

The Esplanade - Central Promenade

Queens Promenade - Derby Castle

Marina, formerly Government House, the Castle Mona, built as a home for the Duke of Athol but, by then a hotel. The road gradually moved away from the sea as it approached the northern end of Douglas Bay, with various buildings and a house on its seaward side, while on the land side towards the bottom of Burnt Mill Hill there were quarry workings. The road continued up Burnt Mill Hill towards Onchan.

A gentleman by the name of Thomas Lightfoot, born in Carbrook on 4 November 1814, retired to the Island in 1870. Lightfoot lived at Athol House, near Little Switzerland, the site now occupied by the Picadilly Court apartments. Despite having retired and moved away, Lightfoot won a contract to build a Horse Tramway in Sheffield in 1872, the first section opening in 1873.

The first half of the 1870s saw much development along the now Promenades, some of these buildings still survive while others have given way to the modern apartment blocks. The Iron Pier opposite the bottom of Broadway was completed in 1869, Victoria Street was completed in 1875, the new Loch Promenade just a few

months later on 9 June 1875. This essentially created what we now know as Douglas Promenade, stretching from Victoria Pier to Burnt Mill Hill.

Thomas Lightfoot was quick to establish the possibility of a Horse Tramway along the now considerable length of the Promenade. He lodged his first proposal with the Rolls Office in Douglas on 27 November 1875 under the title 'Loch Promenade and Douglas Street Tramways, Isle of Man, 1875', for a tramway from the then new Peveril Hotel, now the site of Peveril Buildings, and the bottom of Burnt Mill Hill. With local support Lightfoot promoted an Act of Tynwald: The Douglas Bay Tramway Act was read before Tynwald on 6 June 1876 and received Royal Assent on 12 August.

Meanwhile, confident of his success in being permitted to build the tramway, Lightfoot had begun ordering materials, horse harnesses, and rails and chairs.

The Act specified that the gauge had to be 3 foot and that the width of the trams could not extend further that 21 inches from the outer surface of the wheels and that only animal power could be used. Each horse was to carry a

Tram Nos. 49 and 47, with No. 11 just visible, are stored adjacent to the bus depot buildings at Banks Circus, prior to these buildings being demolished to make way for a Tesco supermarket. September 1993. (AUTHOR)

Approaching the Sea Terminal is horse Keith with Royal tram No. 44 with the Regent Street traffic lights in the background. The area seen in the left of the picture awaits development. (AUTHOR)

bell and after dark the cars should have a red light on the front and a green light on the rear.

The *Manx Sun* of Saturday 10 June 1876 and *Isle of Man Times* reported that a small ceremony was held outside the offices of Mr Lightfoot on the Crescent, when Mr A.W. Adams, Thomas Lightfoot's advocate who had guided the Tramway Bill through the legal process, raised a pickaxe and cut a small square in the tarmac to begin the construction of the tramway.

A single-track line with passing loops was constructed with 35lb/yd rail, the centre walkway for the horses being laid with small stones and tar. The Starbuck Car & Wagon Co. Ltd, later G.F. Milnes & Co., delivered one single-deck tram Number 1 and two double-deck tramcars, Numbers 2 and 3, which arrived on the PS *Tynwald* on Tuesday 1 August. Only one of the double-deck cars was actually operated on opening day, hauled by two horses.

A couple of months after the start of construction, the Public Highway Surveyor, James Garrow, completed his inspection of the line and it opened, without ceremony, between Burnt Mill

Hill (now known as Summer Hill) and the Iron Pier, situated opposite the bottom of Broadway, on 7 August 1876. The first tram was driven by Jack Davies from Onchan.

The Mona's Herald of 16 August reported on the opening, commenting that 'The spirited projector and proprietor, Mr Lightfoot is deserving of much commendation and encouragement for the venture; which is, whether it obtains it or not, deserving of eminent success'.

In the same edition of the paper an advertisement was placed:

* * * * *

DOUGLAS BAY TRAMWAY
THE CARS ARE NOW RUNNING DAILY (Sundays excepted), about every half hour, from BURNT MILL HILL to the PROMENADE, THE FIRST CAR LEAVING Burnt Mill Hill at about 8am, and the last leaving the Promenade about 10pm.

* * * * *

The tramway operated with a stud of 15 horses, stabled at Thomas Lightfoot's private residence, Athol House, that was situated near to the current Queens Hotel. The sea front walled garden was also used as a depot for the three trams. Thomas Lightfoot had purchased Athol House on 20 December 1875 from S.K. Thorburn of Newcastle-upon-Tyne, who in turn had inherited the property.

The remainder of the new line from Iron Pier to Peveril Hotel was completed by 19 December 1876, permission was sought from Governor Loch to open, with an inspection by Captain Richard Penketh MHK JP taking place on 1 January 1877. The report commented that the line had been built in a substantial and workmanlike manner, and while there were a couple of small issues regarding the severity of a curve at the Lifeboat House and the relocation of the Iron Pier loop, the approval was received from Government House on 31 January 1877 and the second stretch of the tramway opened that same day.

After experiments with just one horse, public opinion obliged the operators to continue to use two horses on the double-deck tramcars.

Within three years the whole of the Promenades had been built up and the Derby Castle Pavilion Dance Hall opened in 1877. Later in 1877

Lightfoot purchased three terraced houses at the foot of Summerhill that became known as Tramway Terrace and built new larger stables behind them – the stables that are still in use today.

Lightfoot purchased other establishments in Douglas, and built the Regal Cinema and Grand Hotel,

An interesting view of the three terraced houses purchased by Thomas Lightfoot in 1877, taken in January 1966. The stables are situated behind these buildings, the main entrance being the large double doors to the left. The Crescent Post Office closed many years ago; the buildings housing the newsagents have been demolished, the space providing a small yard and additional access to the stables. (MANX NATIONAL HERITAGE)

but financial issues surrounding the construction of these led Thomas Lightfoot to sell his entire tramway to three local businessmen who in turn created Isle of Man Tramways Ltd, with its office at 46 Athol Street. In order to increase capacity, the new company applied to add four passing loops or sidings. Two were completed in 1883, and a further one in 1884.

Separately the Isle of Man Railway, or an individual or organisation on their behalf, proposed a new tramway from the Isle of Man Railway station to Victoria Pier and applied to the town commissioners on 18 December 1882. This scheme had first emerged in 1878 and did so at intervals, but without success. It is perhaps interesting to note here that in the 'Douglas 2000' plan

A very early photograph of two double deck cars at the Iron Pier, likely taken on opening day in 1876. Car No. 3 is facing north while No. 2 has arrived from Derby Castle. It is interesting to note that No. 2 is in the hands of two horses. Thomas and Jane Lightfoot are on the upper deck, while their youngest son is leaning against Car No. 3 with the conductor's bag. Manager H Leadbetter is holding onto the front handrail on car No. 2. (MANX NATIONAL HERITAGE)

this idea was considered again but as an extension to the Bay Horse Tramway.

Isle of Man Tramways applied for an extension at the north end to the Derby Castle Pleasure Grounds on 17 January 1883, and although approved, was not completed for another seven years.

A further tram was added in 1882, two more in 1883 and a further two, costing £250 0s 0 d each in 1884. Additionally tram Number 1, delivered

as single-deck was converted to double-deck in 1884.

Over 350,000 passengers enjoyed a ride on the line in 1885 and two more single-deck trams, Numbers 9 and 10 were added. Sadly none of these original cars have survived.

During 1883 land had been purchased for a new terminus and depot adjoining the shore at Burnt Mill Hill, the line was diverted off Queens Promenade to the new terminus on the seaward side of the Promenade at Burnt Mill Hill and renamed Derby Castle, despite being somewhat short of the entrance to Derby Castle Pleasure

Tram No. 39 bought in 1902 for £65/0/0, with wheels and axles charged as extra, is seen here passing the Shore Road Shops with an unidentified horse. The shops that included a snack bar and hairdressers, the Manx Kipper Depot and a confectioners and postcard seller, were demolished in the mid 1960s to allow widening of the Promenade. The properties of Clarence Terrace that front the Promenade today were hidden behind the shops. (MANX NATIONAL HERITAGE)

Grounds. Athol House and the depot were sold off by 31 January 1885, although the new building was not completed until a couple of years later.

In 1886 the company applied to lengthen the loop at Falcon Cliff and add two further loops, one on Loch Promenade and a further one at Castle Mona. It is not clear if all these loops were actually added as by 1887 the track had been doubled along Loch Promenade and from Falcon Cliff to Derby Castle. It was to be another 20 years before the line was double track throughout its length.

1887 was a busy year for the company with the purchase of six second-hand double-deck trams from South Shields, bringing the total fleet to 17 trams. All 17 took part in the ceremony to mark the opening of the double-track section. In 1888, 550,000 passengers were carried and 79,278 tram miles covered.

Twenty-six tramcars were in service by 1891 following the delivery of eight toastrack single-deck trams, followed by three very elegant single-deck enclosed cars in 1892.

Protracted negotiations between

Opposite:

Photographs taken from the air are always fascinating but until recently involved chartering a small aircraft or helicopter. However, the modern drone offers a more readily available supply of such pictures. Here we see the Horse Tramway stables with the cliffs behind and the properties of Little Switzerland above.
(JON WORNHAM)

various land owners and the company eventually allowed the tramway to be extended from Burnt Mill Hill to within a few metres of the Pleasure Ground entrance by 1892.

Development of the Promenade had gathered pace during the late 1880s, widening having taken place on Queens Promenade and at Strathallan Crescent.

Thomas Lightfoot died at Birkdale near Southport on 10 January 1893 aged 78, and was buried in Onchan four days later. Eight months later The Douglas & Laxey Coast Electric Tramway Co. opened the first stage of what is now the Manx Electric Railway, from Derby Castle to Groudle. The electric tramway terminus at Derby Castle, just 15ft away from the horse tram terminus, brought even more passengers to the Horse Tramway. Dismantling of the landmark Iron Pier at the bottom of Broadway began on 20 February 1894; the 900ft long structure still in good enough condition to be sold for re-use in Aberystwyth.

The Douglas & Laxey Coast Electric Tramway Co. began negotiations to purchase the Horse Tramway, the idea was leaked to the local press in December 1893, and the sale was completed in April 1894 for £38,000. The Douglas & Laxey Coast Electric Tramway Co. was renamed to Isle of Man Tramways and Electric Power Co. (IOMT&EP Co.) later the same year. The deal to buy the Horse Tramway required them to construct a cable tramway to Upper Douglas. The new cable line ran from Victoria Street to Broadway and opened in 1896.

The continued expansion of Douglas brought about an Act of Tynwald, The Douglas Corporation Act, in 1895, with the new entity taking over from the town commissioners in 1896.

In 1895 work had commenced on the new 12 road tram depot at Derby Castle with a traverser system, with two traversers, one of which came from the previous Burnt Mill Hill shed, to move cars from track to track, and had capacity for 36 trams. The depot is still in use today, although in June 2018 planning permission was received to replace the failing building with a replica. A cast-iron canopy, complete with clock tower, over the Horse Tramway terminal, sadly demolished as unsafe in 1980, was also built at this time.

Harris Promenade in the late nineteenth century with the Sefton Hotel and Gaiety Theatre on the left and the public shelter erected by the then Town Commissioners in 1892. This view, like so many, has changed considerably and is about to again as part of the Douglas Promenades reconstruction scheme, due for completion in 2021 at a cost of £25 Million. (MANX NATIONAL HERITAGE)

The offices on top of the shed were not added until 1935 and for a long time were home to what is now Isle of Man Transport. Since the latter's departure to Banks Circus a conference suite has been operated by Douglas Corporation.

The new owners purchased a further batch of six new trams in 1896, known as the sunshade type, basically a toastrack with a fixed roof. These were numbered 32 to 37 and brought the total number of trams to 37. The timetable advert for 1896 showed the service as:

* * * * *

DOUGLAS BAY HORSE SECTION
A service of Horse Cars will run every few minutes between the Electric Tramway Station and Victoria pier,

starting from the Tramway Station in the morning in time to catch the Fleetwood, Barrow and Liverpool Steamers, the Last Car leaving Derby Castle at pm, and Victoria Street at 11-20pm.

On Sundays the First Car will leave Tramway Station at 9-15am, and Victoria-street at 9-30am; the Last Car leaving the Tramway Station at 10pm, and Victoria-street at 10-15pm.

FARE: TWOPENCE EACH WAY

* * * * *

The IOMT&EP Co. had discussions with the new Douglas Corporation regarding possible electrification of the tramway in 1897 when, following completion of the last piece of double track, over 1.5 million passengers were carried, this rising to over 1.6 million in 1898. The company also considered tramways to other parts of Douglas.

The Isle of Man Tramways & Electric Power Co. had been heavily reliant on Dumbells Bank to finance construction of the coastal tramway and the Upper Douglas Cable Car System, so when Dumbells collapsed on 3 February 1900 the Tramway Company, described as in a shaky state anyway, was forced into liquidation. The affairs of the company were in such chaos that it took until July 1901 for a catalogue of assets to be

A view of Douglas Promenade taken from the Falcon Cliff Hotel, dated late 1880s but likely to be a little earlier as there are no apparent tram tracks. The Castle Mona Hotel is in the right foreground while Derby Terrace, The Esplanade and Clarence Terrace are visible on the right and The Iron Pier on the left. The view from the same spot today would be a little different... (MANX NATIONAL HERITAGE)

compiled. Douglas Corporation was owed just short of £2,000 in royalties for 1900, representing around one tenth of its annual income. In September 1901 the Manx Chancery accepted a £50,000 offer from Douglas Corporation to purchase the Horse Tramway and Upper Douglas Cable Car system.

DOUGLAS CORPORATION
TAKES OVER

The Corporation officially took over on 2 January 1902 and, by way of a ceremony, a cable car left Avondale Road and a horse car left Derby Castle, meeting at the Jubilee clock at 10.40am. Travel was free until noon on

Crowds surround three unidentified double deck trams on Loch Promenade on the occasion of the takeover by Douglas Corporation, on 2 January 1902. The picture was taken before the Promenade was widened to accommodate the flower gardens and walkway. (MANX NATIONAL HERITAGE)

A late nineteenth century picture of Victoria Pier, taken around 2:50pm, shows a vast number of Steam Packet vessels and no less than seven trams on the pier. The tram nearest the camera is No. 1 as a double deck, dating the picture to between 1884 and 1900. (MANX NATIONAL HERITAGE)

Opposite: Passing the foot of Summerhill, formerly Burnt Mill Hill, an unidentified horse hauls tram No. 36 towards the Sea Terminal on 29 April 2018. (AUTHOR)

the day, although a few travellers were upset to discover that the deadline affected incomplete journeys. The Corporation set up a Tramways Committee to look after the two lines.

At the time of the takeover 36 cars, numbered 2 to 37, now operated on the Horse Tramway: 13 double-deckers, 3 single-deck saloons, 14 open toastracks and 6 roofed toastracks, motive power being provided by 68 horses. The track, stable buildings and recently

constructed Strathallan car shed were included in the sale. The 36 trams filled the depot but a new office took up part of one of the tracks and an order for three new trams meant that some cars were again stored at the Brig or the York Road Cable Tramway depot, being transferred to York Road via the cable tramway tracks.

An agreement between the new Tramways Committee and the IOM Harbours Commissioners allowed for

An interesting view of the former No.1 Strathallan Crescent, known as the Brig. The site is now the site of the Kaye Memorial Garden that was completed in 1955. The garden is also now home to a memorial to the victims of the Summerland fire of August 1973. Barron's Groceries and Wines were clearly keen to ensure that their product was well advertised. (AUTHOR'S COLLECTION)

an extension from Peveril Square into Victoria Pier, the new tracks being laid in May 1902. Three new trams were ordered from Milnes bringing the fleet to 39, and a further two in 1905.

In January 1906 the Manx Electric Railway Company approached the Corporation with the intent to electrify the Horse Tramway, in return for royalty payments equal to the average net profit for the previous three years, in order to provide a through service from Ramsey to Victoria Pier, but this was again rejected, as was a further approach in 1908. Interestingly the Corporation itself looked at electrification and the possibility of new lines up to Peel Road and Circular Road via North Quay.

A further two trams arrived in 1907 and another in 1908.

In 1909 it was ruled that a maximum of eight return journeys were to be operated by each horse in the course of a day. Further new trams arrived, Number 46 in 1909 and Number 47 in 1911.

A brief strike occurred on 10 July 1911 following a 'discussion' between a group of cable tramway staff, resulting in them leaving the Corporation or, in their words, being dismissed from employment. As a result both lines were closed that day, the group returning to work that evening having secured a settlement regarding pay and conditions.

The Corporation then ordered an additional single-deck saloon in 1913, to replace the original Number 1, scrapped a few years earlier. The new Number 1 cost £252 3s 6d and was one of the very last trams built at GC Milnes & Voss Co Ltd, the works closing later the same year. That brought the total tram fleet to 47.

The tramway survived the First World War, operating a winter schedule as the holiday industry inevitably slumped. Douglas was described as

Tram No. 43 is moved away from Derby Castle by an unidentified horse with a season opening tram in the early 1970s. (MANX NATIONAL HERITAGE)

becoming a ghost town, Cunninghams Camp and other suitable areas being requisitioned as internment camps. Despite occurring during the war, there was a bread strike on the Island in July 1918, caused by the withdrawal of flour subsidy, pushing the price of a 9d loaf to 1 shilling. The strike took place on 4 and 5 July and had the desired effect as the 9d loaf was re-instated. The Horse Tramway, Cable Tramway and Manx Electric Railway were all affected as was the Steam Packet. However, by 1920 business was picking up again, with 44 cars available for service.

Motor buses were introduced along the Promenade for the first time in 1926 and it was proposed that they would eventually take over from the tramway. The 7.5 minute winter service continued through until 2 November 1927 when, after almost 50 years

Tram No. 47 passes the former Grand Hotel, Yates' Wine Lodge and Jubilee clock at 15:50 on an afternoon in May 1965. Both the businesses are closed but the building does survive as offices. The tram also survives but is out of service and stored off the tramway. (MANX NATIONAL HERITAGE)

24

A busy scene at Derby Castle on 29 July 2016, with tram Nos. 43, 42 and 44 awaiting departure with Philip at the helm. The Terminus Tavern is on the left while the tracks of the Manx Electric Railway are to the right. (CADE WILLIAMSON)

Riding on the upper deck of Tram No. 18 offers the opportunity to capture images of passing trams from a different viewpoint. Queens Promenade is the location for this passing of an unidentified tram heading for Derby Castle in May 1991. (AUTHOR)

Another view, during May 1991, from the upper deck of No. 18, this time taken from the other side and offering a different view of the approaching tram. The rounded roof of the Gaiety Theatre and the Villa Marina are visible ahead. (AUTHOR)

unbroken service, the tramway closed for the winter, however, 2.5 million passengers were carried. Since then only a seasonal service has operated, usually May until September, extended to be April to November in recent years.

Further widening of the Harris and Loch Promenades began around the same time, although not completed until 1934, while doubts surrounded the future of the Horse Tramway. However, in December 1933, the Corporation received the first estimates on the cost of reconstruction of the Horse Tramway.

The relay programme was to use 65lb/yd 'wineglass' rail which would last 40 years, thus assuring the tramway of a future. The Promenade works and the relay of the tramway were completed by 1935, this including a realignment of the tracks from the War Memorial to Greensill's corner. The Horse Tramway had made a profit of £8,000 in 1933 compared with a loss of £4,280 on the bus services, a pattern that continued for several decades.

Three more tramcars, the last cars built for the line and indeed the last horse trams built for anywhere in the

Tram No. 20 prepares for departure from Derby Castle with a good load of passengers in 1934. The Jacobs Biscuits advertisement above the tram shed was lost when the upper floor was added in 1935. (AUTHOR'S COLLECTION)

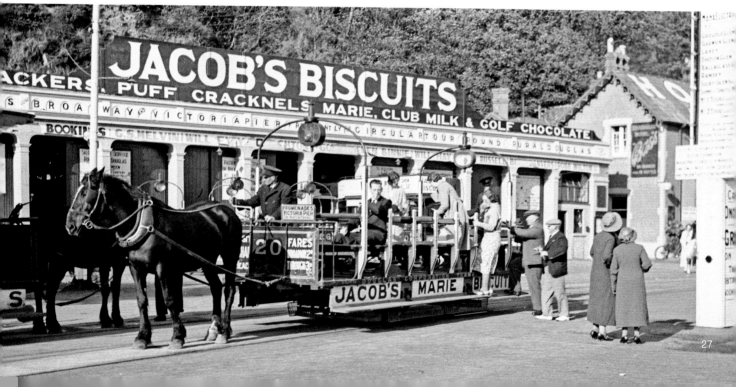

27

Tram No. 47 at the Sea Terminal end of the line. No. 47 was the last conventional toastrack tram to be built for the line, emerging from the works of Milnes Voss & Co in 1911. It was withdrawn from service in 1978 but survives on the Island. (AUTHOR'S COLLECTION)

United Kingdom, were added in 1935 and were of a unique design, being convertible from open to closed, and quickly becoming known as the tomato boxes. Meanwhile, roller bearings were fitted to the existing fleet and the number of horses had reached 135. The high number of horses resulted in stabling at several locations – the Brig was used as was the Queens Hotel and a premises in Fort Street adjoining St Barnabas Church.

In November 1934 plans were approved for the addition of offices at Derby Castle above the then current horse tram depot. The addition of staircases and ground floor offices reduced the number of storage tracks from 12 to 9, thus reducing the number of trams able to be stored to 27, the whole project being completed during the spring of 1936.

Forty six cars were available for service in 1936, with passenger numbers reaching a massive 2.75 million in 1938. During the 1930s the first 'Tram Stop' signs appeared along the Promenade, the signs having red and black lettering on a yellow ochre background, matching the Douglas

Inset left:: A general 1965 view of the Sea Terminal from Loch Promenade shows horse tram No. 10 departing from Victoria Pier running wrong line as far as the crossover immediately under the horse. The former shelters on Victoria Pier are clearly visible, the middle one completed in 1961 as a terminus for the tramway. Sadly both shelters have been demolished to make way for car parking. A Douglas Corporation Regent V approaches the Sea Terminal while no less than three Steam Packet vessels await departure to ports on adjacent islands. (MANX NATIONAL HERITAGE)

Corporation bus stops. These survived until the 1970s when the standard sign became black on white depicting a roofed crossbench car and the words 'Horse Tram Stop'.

Following the outbreak of the Second World War in September 1939, the trams operated until 30 September but did not re-open in the spring of 1940. All the horses were sold and the tramcars were put into store at Derby Castle, York Road and the Brig yard. Many of the seafront hotels, and indeed the tramway stables, were requisitioned to house prisoners of war and internees, and barbed wire fences were erected between the tracks to create secure compounds. Many of the fence postholes are still identifiable by the tarmac squares visible between the tracks.

Following the end of hostilities the Tramways Committee, at its meeting on 18 July 1945, considered the re-opening of the tramway. The ornate tramway shelter at Derby Castle was refurbished and in November 1946 the decision,

A commercial postcard view of Harris Promenade with 4 trams visible and a distinct lack of cars. No. 22 heads towards the Sea Terminal having just passed No. 12 heading north to Derby Castle. Two other trams are following No. 22. The beach is being well used, as are the trams. (AUTHOR'S COLLECTION)

DOUGLAS, I.O.M., THE HARRIS PROMENADE   V5608 possibly one of the most important decisions ever made in relation to the tramway, was made to re-open the tramway for the 1946 season.

In April 1946, 42 horses arrived from Ireland, the stables were derequisitioned and the majority of the tramcars emerged from store. The re-opening ceremony was performed on 22 May by Sir Geoffrey Bromet, the Lieutenant Governor of the Island. A reduced service was operated due, in part, to the limited number of horses but this meant that the number of motor buses operating increased to cover the shortfall in capacity. At the end of the 1946 season, the Corporation was able to compare the relative costs against revenue between buses and horse trams. While the trams showed considerably less profit, the full council referred the matter back to the Tramways Committee who decided to continue the tramway services for 1947 but without adding to the number of horses available. A public meeting in March 1947 produced a vote 5 to 1 in favour of retaining the tramway, while the MSPCA reported on the welfare of the horses, giving a favourable report on

their working conditions. Sadly 14 of the earlier trams, mainly double-deck, were broken up around this time, mainly due to campaigners raising concerns about double-deck cars being hauled by just one horse.

Holidaymakers poured back to the Island in 1947, track re-laying resumed and all looked good for the future. The widening of Strathallan Promenade was completed in 1948 having been delayed by the hostilities. It was suggested, in 1949, that open-top buses should replace the trams but fortunately the Corporation took no action in this direction. All but one of the double-deck cars had by now disappeared and

A similar view to that shown in on page 6 but on a somewhat calmer day. At around quarter to Midday, double deck tram No. 1 is heading for Derby Castle, while an unidentified sister car is approaching the southern terminus at the Sea Terminal.
(AUTHOR'S COLLECTION)

A rather empty tram No. 37 is seen passing the Villa Marina on 3 June 2008. Given that there are three staff on the front, it is likely that this is a horse training run. (AUTHOR)

in 1955 the sole survivor (Number 14) left the Island for restoration and preservation, initially stored in the Norwood tram depot before moving to the new Museum of British Transport at Clapham in South London, opened on the site of an old bus depot in 1960.

1956 marked the 80th anniversary of the opening of the tramway. There was a brief ceremony to get the season underway, with the main celebrations being held on 7 August. The horses and trams were assembled at Victoria Pier, the trams being hauled six at a time by a Corporation bus. There was then a procession of trams led by car Number 40, driven by international horsewoman Pat Smythe, towards Derby Castle and then back to the Villa Marina. Mrs D'Echevarria, granddaughter of the tramway founder, Thomas Lightfoot, was also among the guests. The Promenade was lined three or four deep throughout its length, the crowds applauding as the procession of horses and trams passed.

Holiday traffic began to decline towards the end of the 1950s, although 20 new horses were purchased for the 1958 season. 1958 was a very wet

The Horse Tram Experience notice displaying times of operation and fares at Derby Castle in 2006. (AUTHOR)

A stunning image of winter saloon No. 27 at Derby Castle, just after the takeover by Douglas Corporation in 1902, with a roof mounted advertisement board and wording above and below the windows advertising the Manx Electric and Snaefell Mountain Railways. Above the windows it reads- *The Douglas, Laxey, Snaefell Mountain and Ramsey Electric Tramway: Places to Visit along the Way,* while on the side panels below the windows it reads- *Groudle Glen, Laxey, Snaefell Mountain, Bulgham Bay, Dhoon Glen, Glen Mona, Ballaglass, Port Mooar, Lewaigue, Ramsey.* (AUTHOR'S COLLECTION)

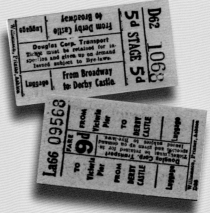

season and passenger numbers dropped, mainly due to the lack of visitors and threats of closure were again rumoured, but promptly officially denied.

During the summer of 1960 plans were unveiled as part of the new Sea Terminal Building project, to include a new bus and tramway terminal.

Tynwald granted permission in 1961 for a fare increase, as the tramway was now regarded as a speciality ride rather than public transport. The season was opened by Mr W.J. Fowler, Chairman of the Light Railway Transport League, with the new terminus on Victoria Pier opening at the same time. This facility gained many favourable comments, although sadly it was little used.

The Fleetwood steamer services ceased after the summer of 1961, resulting in a reduction in the number of day trippers to the Island in 1962.

Her Majesty Queen Elizabeth the Queen Mother visited the Island for Tynwald Day 1964 and rode on the Horse Tramway from Summer Hill to the Villa Marina. Car Number 44 was chosen for the royal passenger and was

specially painted and decorated for the occasion. The stud of horses was 56 at the beginning of 1964, reducing to 43 by the winter. Fifteen new horses were purchased at the beginning of 1965, a year that saw another royal visit, this time by HRH Princess Margaret and Lord Snowdon. Car Number 44 was used again becoming the 'Royal Tram'. During their visit HRH Princess Margaret opened the, by then completed, new Sea Terminal building on 6 July.

Meanwhile the Corporation had purchased the Derby Castle complex in 1964 with plans to demolish the buildings and replace them with a modern leisure facility. The

Tram No. 22 with its unique pitched roof was withdrawn from service and converted into a tram shop in 1978. It is seen here outside the sheds in July 1988, with a nice array of advertising boards around. The entrance to the Terminus Building features a superb example of Art Deco glazing. The notice above the tram indicates that during inclement weather, the shop remains inside the shed. (AUTHOR)

A view that has changed little in the last 25 years, although traffic levels have increased considerably, shows open toastrack tram No. 32 passing the Gaiety Theatre and Sefton Hotel in May 1991. This image makes an interesting comparison with the picture on page 17. (AUTHOR)

Summerland complex was completed in 1970. In order to simplify ticketing, and to encourage an increase in passengers, a flat fare system was introduced in 1966, and had the desired effect on passenger numbers, which was to continue over the next few years. The 1968 to 1971 seasons produced some very reasonable surpluses, this going to make up for some of the losses on the bus services. Such was the situation that at a

Douglas Town Council meeting it was suggested that the buses should be taken over by government, even if that meant giving the buses away.

HRH the Duke of Edinburgh visited the line in 1970, and again in 1972 with Her Majesty the Queen, HRH Princess Anne and Admiral of the Fleet, Earl Mountbatten of Burma. The royal party rode from the new terminus at Victoria Pier to the Sefton Hotel in cars 44 and 36, both specially painted

Tram No. 32 is seen passing the entrance to the now demolished Metropole Hotel, not long after beginning its journey from Derby Castle to the Sea Terminal during May 1989. The Milnes Hotel is now the Regency Hotel but in the same buildings, the Crescent Hotel became the Crescent Leisure Centre but is now closed. (AUTHOR)

Horse Carol brings tram No. 32 into Derby Castle in May 1991. The buildings of Summerhill are visible above the tram. (AUTHOR'S COLLECTION)

The second tram to carry the number 1 was delivered to the Tramway in 1913. It is seen here arriving at the Sea Terminal terminus during May 1986. The new Island in the middle of the road had been added by this time but judging by the Mini, Victoria Street was still two way. The Ford Cortina seems a little the worse for wear. (AUTHOR)

and decked out with flowers. Crowds of well-wishers lined the Promenade, with a large number of locals turning out to see the royal party.

During the early 1970s the Isle of Man Tourist Board had been actively trying to increase the number of visitors to the Island through advertising, which in turn had increased the number of passengers on the Horse Tramway. Renewed local interest sparked by the royal visitors is thought to have contributed as well,

and by 1973 the numbers were heading back up towards those of the early 1920s. The Corporation had bought further new horses from Belfast in early 1971, adding to the 49 already available for the tramway. In 1974 over 1.5 million passengers were carried.

The price of horses showed a sharp increase around this time, resulting in the Corporation starting a breeding programme, with any new foals not working the tramway until they were at least three years old.

A CENTURY OF SERVICE

The Island, like other areas of the British Isles, went through a difficult time in the mid-1970s, with industrial disputes and the ever rising price of oil. The Island's holiday industry was hit further in 1973 with the internationally reported massive fire at the Summerland complex, the Horse Tramway service being curtailed for the rest of that season.

The centenary of the Horse Tramway fell on 7 August 1976 but, as this was a Saturday, the celebrations were held on Monday 9 August, by chance during the author's very first visit to the Island. The Museum of British Transport had closed in 1973 and Douglas Car Number 14 had been stored off display by its now owners, The Science Museum, in London. Negotiations commenced and the Science Museum was persuaded to allow it to return to the Island, arriving here on loan in March 1976, be repainted

On Monday 9 August 1976 a major event celebrated the Centenary of the Horse Tramway. This view shows the horses arriving at the Sea Terminal for a parade and then a cavalcade of trams back to Derby Castle. Victoria Street is seen in the centre of the picture. (MANX NATIONAL HERITAGE)

and take part in the celebrations. Open toastrack Number 12 was also restored to traffic for the centenary and a further batch 1, 10, 21, 27, 28, 29, 30, 34, 35, 36, 37, 38, 40, 42, 44, 46, 47 and 49 all received attention prior to the celebrations. Car Number 44, that was only returned to the depot the evening before, was hauled as was commonplace at the time by a Douglas Corporation double-deck bus, watched by the then much younger author. The stable staff worked through the night grooming the 50 horses, all brass work was meticulously polished and nameboards provided for each horse.

At 10am on the morning of Monday 9 August, the horses were led along the Promenade towards Victoria Pier where the trams were waiting, having been hauled there five at a time

Following the end of the 2014 season the refurbishment of Douglas Promenade was due to get underway and there was real fear that the tramway was not included in the plans at all, or that the tracks would be relocated to the side of the road. Whichever was the case, it was likely that the 14 September 2014 would be the last day of operation on the double track centre of the road alignment. Douglas Corporation therefore arranged a special day, including a parallel run along the front of the Villa Marina. Here we see tram Nos. 18 and 44 making history, the sun even breaking through for the occasion. (AUTHOR)

A view of the cavalcade making its way along Loch Promenade on 9 August 1976, double deck car No. 14 leads Royal car No.44 and nearest the camera is No. 12. The huge crowd that turned out is clearly evident, the road being closed for the event. An interesting array of motor vehicles are parked; Austin Princess, Ford Capri, Commer van, Mini and Austin 1100 among others. (MANX NATIONAL HERITAGE)

A further view of the cavalcade departing from the Sea Terminal, with No. 14 leading. The Jubilee clock is to the right of the picture. It is interesting to note that the coach in the car park at the front of the Sea Terminal is facing north, suggesting that the road there was two way at the time. (MANX NATIONAL HERITAGE)

by a double-decker bus. Then at 11.15am double-deck car Number 14 left Victoria Pier at the head of the procession that also included the newly restored Upper Douglas cable car. Every serviceable tram followed, their passengers being issued with special centenary tickets. It is estimated that 30,000 people lined the Promenade from end to end. Car Number 14 remained at Derby Castle depot, only being used occasionally, until in 1990 it was moved to the Manx Museum in Douglas, where it remains on display to this day.

The tramway was experiencing an ever increasing volume of road traffic as the 1970s grew older and the extension onto Victoria Pier, although little used, was effectively abandoned. During the winter months it was usual to use the tram tracks as car parking.

The debate about the future of the Corporation buses continued and in the summer of 1975 Douglas Corporation agreed to the nationalisation of its bus services, a process that was concluded in 1977.

The millennium of Tynwald was celebrated in 1979 and after much promotion the number of visitors to the Island was higher than in previous years and the tramway carried just over 860,000 passengers during the season.

During 1980 the station canopy at Derby Castle was deemed to have become unsafe, the ravages of the salt spray and age taking their toll. The structure was dismantled and has never been replaced. The tramway operated at a loss in 1980 for the first time in its history, with passenger numbers down to 742,000, and the beginning of what was to be a poor decade with numbers falling, apart from 1983 and 1987 which showed modest increases on 1982 and 1986 respectively. Total passengers for 1989 were down to 264,000 and by 1991 to just short of 180,000.

Car Number 46 spent the summer of 1987 on display in Noble's Park, Douglas before being shipped to the mainland, fully restored and put on display at the Woodside Ferry Terminal in Birkenhead. While double-deck car Number 14 was at Derby Castle its use

was restricted, but the idea of having a working double-deck car led Douglas Corporation to look to converting car Number 18 back to a double-decker. This car had started life in South Shields, coming to the Island as a double-decker in 1887 and being reduced to a single deck in 1903. The project went ahead and the restored car emerged from the workshops in early 1989, painted in an Okell's maroon livery in recognition of the sponsorship by the brewery for the conversion and

Two horse power! The tramway celebrated its 140th birthday on 7 August 2016, and as part of the celebrations tram No. 18 was hauled by two horses for two return trips along the Promenades. Seen here on Loch Promenade with the first of the return journeys is tram No. 18 with horses William and Douglas. (AUTHOR)

An interesting picture of an event on the Centenary day, 9 August 1976. The well decorated tram is about to be pulled the length of the Promenade by the group of seven. Good fun was clearly being had by all. (MANX NATIONAL HERITAGE)

restoration. The tram took part in the 1989 season launch on 30 April. Meanwhile the former Upper Douglas Cable Tramway depot at York Road was demolished in 1988, amidst much criticism. The depot had been used to store and work on Horse Tramway trams and latterly motor buses.

The Douglas Corporation Tramways Committee, more recently known as the Transport Committee, was disbanded in early 1988, responsibility moving to the Entertainment and Publicity Committee. The tramway took over the operation of the beach donkeys for the summer of 1988 in an effort to reverse the losses incurred.

Projected losses during 1990, following actual losses in 1989, led the

Corporation to consider closure or transfer to the Government Department of Tourism & Transport. There had also been a plan in late 1990 to sell off the stables and move the horses to a farm at Pulrose and then transport them by road to the tramway as required.

When the 1992 season began it was firmly believed that it would be the last or at least the penultimate season under Douglas Corporation, a process that we now know took until 2016 to actually happen.

The Manx Electric Railway had its centenary in 1993, the Island celebrating with a 'Year of Railways'. As part of these celebrations the Horse Tramway season started at Easter, somewhat earlier than normal. Fares for the year were set at £1.10 giving unlimited travel for a whole day. Stored cars 11, 47 and 49 were moved from Ramsey MER car sheds to Douglas and placed behind the new steam railway carriage shed in early June 1993. Cars 21 and 38 received a special blue and gold Douglas 2000 livery as part of the promotion for the Douglas 2000 plan.

Mr Wilson Gibb retired as General Manager of the Horse Tramway on 18 August 1993 and was succeeded by Mr Peter Cannan, appointed as Tramway Supervisor. Mr Gibb was invited to drive a tram, the chosen tram Number 44 having 'L' plates attached and suitably decorated with garlands and a banner 'Good Luck Wilson – on your retirement'.

The celebrations for the Manx Electric resulted in a vast number of visiting enthusiasts and took the passenger numbers back over the

An early view along Queens Promenade looking north towards the Derby Castle entertainment complex, with the 1886 tram sheds and station clearly visible. Burnt Mill Hill, now Summerhill, can be seen climbing towards Onchan on the left. (AUTHOR'S COLLECTION)

Open toastrack tram No. 39 passes a somewhat different looking Villa Marina. Pretty much this whole view has changed, the Villa has been extended and the entrance moved, the road has a central island and traffic lights. The tram carries an advert for the event at the Villa and an event at the Palace Lido to be held on 30 July 1965. (MANX NATIONAL HERITAGE)

200,000 mark for that year to 205,061.

The diagonal parking on the seaward side of Loch Promenade was made permanent following some tests carried out in late 1993, and concerns about an increase in accidents were unfounded although there was concern that there may be an attempt to reduce the tramway to single-track on the stretch.

Various suggestions regarding the future of the Horse Tramway were forthcoming, making it single-track and/or moving it onto the Promenade walkway. These suggestions all formed part of a new Douglas 2000 project, looking at Douglas as it moved towards the 21st century. Other options

included extending the tramway round past the Sea Terminal and along North Quay, with a new terminus at the steam railway station.

Car Number 45 was returned to service in 1994 after a few years stored, the operating season reverting to usual, starting in early May and operating through to 1 October.

A safety initiative by new management prevented conductors from riding on the front of the car, thus returning them to the rear platform from where they could observe any issues that arose with the passengers. The long hot spell of 1995 produced a rare event on 29 June when the entire service was operated by fully open toastracks, the first time for many years.

Cars 21 and 30 had their Douglas 2000 livery removed at the end of the 1995 season. During the 1995/96 winter the track at the Sea Terminal end of the line was lifted to allow work on the Island-wide IRIS sewage project to be undertaken. The track was back in place in good time for the commencement of the 1996 season.

During a later stage of this work, in early 2001, two of the original Cable

Tramway cable wheels were unearthed, much to the surprise of the contractors. Thankfully, and in no small part due to the cooperation of the contractors, one of the wheels, that had sat undiscovered for approaching 85 years, was removed complete. After storage for many years the wheel is due to be returned to be displayed near the tramway terminus at the Sea Terminal as part of the Promenade refurbishment plans.

The tramway celebrated its 120 anniversary in 1996, coinciding with the centenary of Douglas Corporation. As part of the celebrations, two trams, Numbers 36 and 43, appeared carrying special illuminations on the ends and sides of the cars, powered by generators mounted on one of the driver platforms. The ends simply showed '1896 – 1996', while the sides 'Douglas 100 Years'.

Despite good loads in the early and mid-evenings, with trams operating until 10pm, the overall Horse Tramway passenger numbers for the 1996 season were disappointing. The evening service proved very worthwhile and was complemented in the mid-summer by an illuminated Manx Electric car

working to Groudle in conjunction with the Groudle Glen Railway, enabling travel by horse, electric and steam all in one evening! The general appearance of the entire horse tram fleet was deemed to have improved under the recently appointed management.

Toastrack car Number 40 was extensively rebuilt during the 1996/1997 winter and re-entered service on 23 July 1997. The all-day ticket for the 1997 season was £1.40 and a four-tram service was operated during the two week TT Festival.

1998 marked the 125th anniversary of the opening of the Douglas to Peel

Royal Tram No. 44 built by the United Electric Car Company in 1907, passes the Castle Mona Hotel in the charge of the Mayor of Douglas during June 1965. Visible over the roof of the tram are the roof of the Palace Ballroom and Falcon Cliff Hotel. (MANX NATIONAL HERITAGE)

47

Toastrack car No. 22 stands outside Derby Castle shed displaying its pitched roof. Delivered in 1890 along with car No. 21, the pair were used during the opening of the Queens Promenade on 8 July 1890. No. 22 had its roof added in 1908, originally it was possible to roll the canvas back on fine days. It retains the roof, although now fixed and mounted on metal framework, to this day. It was converted for use as a shop in 1978. (AUTHOR'S COLLECTION)

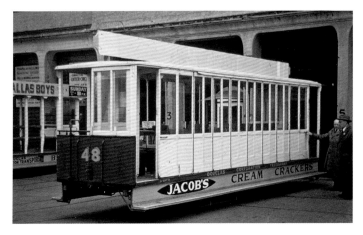

Vulcan car No. 48 is shown with the side doors in the closed position. When running in this format, the end of each seat was folded down to create a corridor down the side of the tram to allow access to the seats. (AUTHOR'S COLLECTION)

steam railway and a year of events under the 'Steam 125' banner. The oldest surviving car, Number 11, was returned to Derby Castle in late 1998 with a plan for restoration to service condition. Number 11 is the sole survivor of the many cars built new for the tramway by the Starbuck Car & Wagon Co. Ltd. Sadly this restoration never got underway. The TT Festival Mad Sunday street party was moved from Loch Promenade to the area at Derby Castle, thus preventing the tramway operating at all on that day, what would have been one of the busiest days of the year.

The 1999 season operated much the same as the previous year. In honour of the memory of Councillor John Harley, the Mayor of Douglas who died following an illness, the tramway and several other departments of the Corporation were closed 3–7 September 1999. On Friday 17 September, with the season drawing to a close, disaster struck on Loch Promenade. The new Tower House shopping centre was under construction and a 25-ton crane had been in use all

Car No. 46 picking up passengers outside the Imperial Hotel on Queens Promenade, with the Castle Mona Hotel visible in the background. Sadly the Imperial has been demolished in recent weeks and the future of the Castle Mona is still uncertain.

(AUTHOR'S COLLECTION)

It was once traditional that there would be an official launch of the Tramway each season. Here we see a ribbon cutting ceremony under the ornate canopy at Derby Castle in May 1973. The Summerland complex behind was to make world news just a few months later as the result of a devastating fire. (MANX NATIONAL HERITAGE)

day. The crane had swung, resulting in the counterweight fouling the tramway. Car 35 was travelling north when it struck the crane, the roof collapsing onto the passengers, resulting in two elderly people being taken to hospital. The horse was unharmed and later walked back to the stables, while the damaged tram was hauled by road vehicle to Derby Castle depot.

Car Number 35, damaged in the collision with the crane, was rebuilt over the winter of 1999/2000, while along the route new red on white 'Tram Stop' signs were installed. During the first half of 2000 the stables received a much needed upgrade. The work provided improved accommodation for the horses, and a new roof and floor were installed along with better drainage. The traditional bays have been replaced with boxes, giving the horses room to lie down between shifts if they wish.

The 125th anniversary of the Horse Tramway was celebrated in 2001, each tram used in service that year receiving a special 125th logo sticker. On the evening of the actual anniversary, 7 August, there was a parade with the Promenade closed to traffic to accommodate the large crowd that gathered. Unlike previous parades the start this time was at Derby Castle where the Mayor, Councillor Stephen Pitts, made his speech alongside the still to be restored car Number 11. Double-deck car 18 led the cavalcade conveying the Lieutenant Governor Air Marshall Ian Macfadyen together with the visiting Governors of Jersey and Guernsey. Car 43 conveyed a party of visiting schoolchildren from the former Soviet

An amazing picture, dating from the mid 1970s, of Loch Promenade at its junction with Victoria Street with Tram No. 47 heading towards Derby Castle and about to pass an unidentified toastrack that has stopped to allow 47 to cross to the landward track. The Jubilee clock sat in the middle of the road at the junction, Victoria Street still two way at this time, and an interesting selection of vehicles complete the scene. (THURSTAN DENNE COLLECTION)

Douglas Corporation issued timetable leaflet for 2015.

In preparation for the Centenary parade on 9 August 1976, the trams were hauled to the Sea Terminal in batches. This impressive line-up consists of Nos. 35, 27, 21, 47, 34, 1 and 49, awaiting their turn in the parade. (THURSTAN DENNE COLLECTION)

Republic. On return to Derby Castle the party transferred to Summerland for a reception where a further speech was made by Betty Quirk, Chair of the Corporation Leisure and Services Committee. An 'adopt a horse' programme was introduced in order to promote the tramway.

A private car parked across the track on the approach to Derby Castle caused nearly half a day's service to be cancelled on 31 August 2002. Services eventually got underway around 1pm.

The 2003 season was shortened as the growing costs of the tramway threatened its future, with the tramway only operating from the beginning of May to the end of September. The tramway was promoted with a number of banners being placed at prominent roadside locations around the town at the start of the 2004 season. The Lieutenant Governor and his family visited the stables on Sunday 2 May to see horse Mark adopted by his family during the 2001 'adopt a horse' scheme.

Douglas Corporation looked at the idea of running some illuminated cars for the run up to Christmas 2004, but sadly the idea never got off the ground.

Douglas Bay Horse Tramway Timetable issued by Isle of Man Railways for the 2017 season.

The tramway was closed along with a large part of the Promenade to accommodate the security required around the Villa Marina for the British Irish Conference on 20 May 2005.

In an attempt to reduce the number of cars left parked across the tracks and outside the depot at Derby Castle, barriers and large 'no parking' signs were put in place.

Only 76,478 passengers travelled on the tramway in 2005, the trams covering around 20,000 miles. This represents a drop of over 100,000 on the 1995 figure with the mileage covered being less than a third of that of 1995.

Despite receiving some cosmetic attention in April and being moved into the depot in May, car Number 11 remained in need of restoration and was moved to the former Homefield bus depot on 21 September 2005 for undercover storage. It was joined by cars 47 and 49. The local fire service had requested the suspension of tramway services along the Promenade during the race periods to reduce traffic congestion. Thankfully the Corporation rejected the request. This would have been bad news for the tramway as like so much of the Island the TT Festival is probably the busiest two weeks of the year.

Open Toastrack tram No. 20 at Derby Castle, photographed before the upper floor was added to the tram sheds in 1935. (AUTHOR'S COLLECTION)

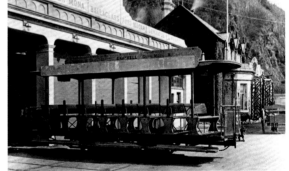

Toastrack tram No. 36 stands outside the shed at Derby Castle sometime around the turn of the 20th century. The advertisement above the shed is promoting the Manx Electric and Snaefell Mountain Tramways. (AUTHOR'S COLLECTION)

The Frank Matcham-designed Gaiety Theatre and the Villa Marina Colonnade provide a background to this view of No. 18 making good progress towards the Sea Terminal in the early 1990s. (AUTHOR)

A line up of toastracks at Derby Castle in 1998. Tram Nos. 38 and 35 await their next duty while No. 36 will soon be heading off to the Sea Terminal. The flagpoles sit in the remains of the supports of the canopy that once covered the tracks here. (AUTHOR)

◀ A very colourful car No. 46 stands outside the shed at Derby Castle. The red, white and blue livery was originally applied in 1947, the addition of a Union Jack on the roof for the Festival of Britain was completed in 1951. (AUTHOR'S COLLECTION)

After the success of the local Commonwealth Games team in Australia, Douglas Corporation provided double-deck horse tram Number 18, instead of an open-top bus, to convey the athletes and officials along the Promenade from the Sea Terminal to the Villa Marina for a reception on 20 April 2006.

Fares for the 2006 season were reduced to £1.00 single and the all-day tickets were withdrawn, a move intended to encourage more passengers to use the tramway.

It was suggested that a spare Horse Tramway car should be put on static display on the short length of cable tramway track laid at the bottom of Victoria Street, but potential damage to the car by late night revellers resulted in the idea being shelved.

One of the new type Horse Drawn Tram cars supplied to Douglas Corporation by The Vulcan Motor & Engineering Co. (1906) Ltd., Crossens, Southport. No.1922.

An official picture of Vulcan built tram No. 48, supplied to the Tramway in 1935, at Derby Castle. In the background work is underway on the upper floor of the tram sheds that were added the same year. (AUTHOR'S COLLECTION)

Having completed three quarters of a mile of the 1.6 mile route, Mark has a well loaded tram No. 33 in tow on Queens Promenade on 20 August 2008. (AUTHOR)

A further threat to the future of the Horse Tramway came when the Corporation announced that it needed to cut overall expenses by £180,000. However, the tramway survived the cuts and the 2007 season produced little change to the service, although car 36 did return to traffic after a number of years absent.

However, since the end of the 2007 season, the tramway has been the subject of much discussion. The hidden cost of clearing up after the horses was raised at a Corporation meeting and the possibility of the horses wearing nappies was considered! More worrying was an idea to remove the conductors from the trams and then operate non-stop between Derby Castle and Sea Terminal. It seems unlikely that health and safety inspectors would approve operating without a conductor.

In January 2008 it was announced that the tramway had lost £270,000 the previous year and that the 2008 season would be shortened by four weeks, starting in mid-May and finishing in mid-September. The only change implemented was the reduction in the operating season.

At the December meeting of the Borough Council, members were told that the operating deficit for the 2008 season had been reduced by £20,000 despite a further reduction in passenger numbers.

At the same meeting came the news that for the 2009 season the trams would start later in the morning at 11am and continue into the evening, finishing at 8pm. The Council Leader gave his backing to keeping the trams, at that meeting, adding that the lack of the Summerland complex or a replacement attraction was a factor in the passenger reductions. However, the later start prevented intending Manx Electric Railway passengers from using

the tramway to reach Derby Castle for the early departures to Laxey, Ramsey and Snaefell.

The double-deck tram was out in service every day, occasionally more than once, and generally the season went well, although the later service coupled with higher fares did push some intending passengers away and the passenger figure for the year showed a decrease. The biggest break from the norm came towards the end of the year with the announcement that Santa trams would run in the week running up to Christmas.

The tramway staff decorated tram Number 1 with lights inside and out

A pair of refurbished tram wheels await fitting in June 2014. The trams are fitted with roller bearings making them light work for the horses. (AUTHOR)

and provided some appropriate horse names. The Manx Electric Derby Castle ticket office became Santa's Grotto, where the younger generations could visit Santa and receive a gift. The operation was a resounding success with all trams booked up in advance and the weather obliged with sunshine on all three days. The success of the operation introduced the idea of corporate charters and events being considered.

The results from the experiment of starting later and finishing later meant that for the following season the early start would be re-introduced.

In early 2010, two of the trams were moved from Derby Castle shed to the new Jurby Transport Museum. Car 22, the former tram shop, was to see further use as a shop at Jurby, while the former Upper Douglas Cable Car was to be an exhibit at the new museum. A short while later, cars 11, 47 and 49 also went to Jurby from the former Homefield bus depot that was being emptied in preparation for sale of the building.

The 2010 season started on 10 May and a new innovation saw the introduction of Horse Tramway Experience days. The day included a

visit to the stables, assisting with the preparation and welfare of the horses, a tour of the tram sheds and a trip along the line.

The Santa trams were repeated for 2010, with eight days of operation instead of the six the previous year.

The Corporation approved the movement of car Number 35 to the Home of Rest for Old Horses on Richmond Hill. The car is displayed within a fenced area on a short length of track. The 2011 season was extended at the end of the season to accommodate the additional passengers associated with the holding of the Commonwealth Youth games on the Island. An attractive four-page timetable and information leaflet was produced for the season and has appeared each year since.

A towable poop scooper was purchased in 2011 to assist in keeping the Promenade clear of horse droppings.

Towards the end of that year the state of the Promenade and its upgrading was back on the agenda. Previous discussions had come to nothing but the position of the Horse Tramway and/or whether it should be retained at all prompted many opinions to be expressed.

Over the next few years the discussions continued: the repositioning of the tramway onto the promenade walkway was one suggestion or simply moving it to the seaward side of the roadway was another.

During 2013 a short section of the Loch Promenade and Peveril Square was refurbished utilising modern stonework with a tarmac resurface of the road. This work included a new island alongside the current Sea Terminal tramway terminus. The intention was to continue with this work, recommencing in Autumn 2014, following the end of the tramway season, although there had still not been a firm decision about the position or overall future of the tramway.

During May Douglas Councillor Stephen Pitts said that the tramway was well worth keeping as it was a popular attraction. However, fears for its future

Detail of one of the boards hanging from the frames over the ends of tram No. 42. (AUTHOR)

The Douglas Corporation fares notice displayed in a tram. (AUTHOR)

Christmas Specials

Douglas Corporation joined in with the Christmas festivities for 2009 and operated 'Santa' trams. On 19 December 2009 tram No. 1 leaves the Sea Terminal with Rudolf in charge, and is seen here approaching Regent Street. (AUTHOR)

A view inside the well decorated tram No. 1. A small generator was attached under the tram to power the lights. (AUTHOR)

In splendid evening light, Rudolf heads along Queens Promenade on Saturday 19 December 2009, with another group of children who have just met Santa at Derby Castle. (AUTHOR)

The Santa trams were crewed by two of the tramway stalwarts, captured posing with horse Rudolf at Derby Castle. (AUTHOR)

The 2011 Santa trams were operated by Tram No. 1 equally well decorated. As evening falls the external decorative lighting is shown off to good effect, with even the tram number cleverly lit. (AUTHOR)

were commonplace and in anticipation that 2014 would be the last season that the tramway would run along the centre of the Promenade, with many actually believing that it would be the last season ever, Douglas Corporation organised a special final weekend, culminating in a final trip using the double-deck tram hauled by Mark, with the Mayor and Mayoress of Douglas overseeing the proceedings. It was an emotional weekend, with many hundreds of people both local and visitors making a trip along the line. The stables were open to the public for

the day and piles of old horse shoes were given away, while out on the line a parallel run was performed with cars 18 and 44 running side by side along the front of the Villa Marina. There were some tearful eyes as tram Number 18 was pushed into the shed after completion of the final trip.

The work on the Promenade was due to start within a week or two but, in early October, the Minister for the Department of Infrastructure announced that the plans were shelved as he was not satisfied that the proposed work was the correct way forward.

The Manx Electric Railway celebrated its 125th Anniversary on 7 September 2018. As part of a week of celebrations a party was held at Laxey station on Sunday 2 September. One of the features was the lining up of Douglas Bay Horse Tramway tram No. 1 dating from 1913, Manx Electric Railway No. 1 dating from 1893 and Snaefell Mountain Railway No. 1 dating from 1895. The trio are seen here with horse Douglas. (AUTHOR)

Horse William passing the Villa Marina on 13 May 2018 with restored tram No. 45. This tram has had a central roof mounted advertisement board added that, when photographed, was awaiting an advert. The board does allow long distance identification of the tram. (AUTHOR)

Therefore, as a result of the postponement of the Promenade works, the Tramway re-opened at the beginning of the 2015, its 139th season, as usual. The discussion around the refurbishment of the Promenade and position of the tramway was regularly in the news, and, while there were objectors, a large proportion of the comments were in support of the tramway.

The government released a revised plan for the entire Promenade, on 6 May 2015, with the tramway on the walkway from around half way, a plan that immediately met with severe objection, and a major campaign was begun to keep the tramway off the walkway.

Such was the reaction that a public enquiry was held over three days in late November, the daytime sessions being supplemented by evening sessions to allow those working to put their views to the Inspector.

The enquiry was at times farcical, with the various 'experts' failing to sufficiently answer the points raised by

One crown coin produced for the Centenary in 1976. (AUTHOR'S COLLECTION)

the probably larger than expected numbers that attended. One specific was when a 'consultant traffic engineer' was unable to calculate that a vehicle moving at 20mph, would take four and a half minutes to cover one and a half miles.

CORPORATION ANNOUNCES CLOSURE

Santa trams operated again for Christmas 2015 and in early January the timetable plans for the 2016 season were announced, including a note that there would be some special events to mark the 140th anniversary of the tramway. However at a special meeting on Thursday 21 January 2016, the Douglas Borough Council voted, after lengthy discussion, to terminate the service and that the tramway would not operate during 2016. In what appeared to be a further blow, the government announced that it would proceed with plans to reconstruct the Promenade but without including the tramway tracks.

One of the TT traditions is the Fair on the Douglas Promenade Walkway, seen here with horse Torrin and tram No. 45 passing. The Douglas War Memorial stands proud to the left of the tram. (AUTHOR)

This came as a direct result of the Douglas Corporation decision. Perhaps not surprisingly, negotiations and discussions between various heritage groups, Isle of Man Railways and Manx National Heritage, were instigated almost immediately. While it seemed likely that a short-term reprieve would be successful, the longer term retention of the tramway was less secure.

On 22 March 2016 the government announced that it had upheld the decision and recommendations of the public enquiry, and that the proposal to move the tramway onto the walkway for around half its distance had been abandoned. A few days later, on 26 March, came the news that the talks between the various groups and government departments had resulted in an agreement that Isle of Man Railways would operate the line for the 2016, 2017 and 2018 seasons, as part of the heritage railway portfolio. This renewed hope for the future, given the very positive developments on the other railways under the current Director of Public Transport.

With very little delay, and as might have been expected, the tram fleet was

With TT over, the roads on the Island are beginning to quieten down as horse Torrin passes the Villa Marina with tram No. 45 on 10 June 2018. (AUTHOR)

tidied up, Horse Tramway GO cards were introduced, and a full timetable leaflet published. Trams operated from 30 April through until 30 October, the longest operating season for many years. The Douglas Corporation name was quickly removed as the rebranding back to 'The Douglas Bay Horse Tramway' accelerated, with new 'Tram Stop' signs and new titles on the trams themselves. Bushy's Brewery, a local producer, supported the campaign to retain the trams with a special design for its TT2016 merchandise.

The 140th anniversary was celebrated on Sunday 7 August with a series of events including two horses on the double-deck tram and a cavalcade towards the end of the day, with a line-up of trams along the front of the Villa Marina.

Passenger numbers for the season were up by over 40% from 49,000 in 2015 to over 69,500 in 2016.

Meanwhile, following the acceptance of the findings of the public enquiry, the Department of Infrastructure announced in April 2016 that it had revised the plans for the Promenade but without the tramway track south of the Villa Marina. Included in the plan was a potential space for the tramway that

On the first Sunday of the 2018 operating season, horse Keith has refurbished tram No.36 for the return journey to the Sea Terminal. (AUTHOR)

would be re-instated at a later date.

This suggestion was challenged by various groups as being against The Douglas Promenades Conservation Area Order 2002 that stated: 'Synonymous with the image of the Promenades is the unique system of horse trams. It is judged that this feature makes an important contribution to the special character of the Conservation Area'.

In July 2016 the Department of Infrastructure published a 19 page document 'Proposals Regarding the Future Operation of Douglas Bay Horse Tramway'. This document made a long list of recommendations including:

1. That Tynwald supports the Department of Infrastructure operating the Douglas Bay Horse Tramway for 2017 and 2018.

2. That the business case for continuation of the Tramway and a new combined facility on the site of either the Strathallan tram depot or Derby Castle continue to be evaluated during the 2017 and 2018 Tramway operations.

3. That a new single line Tramway track be laid from Derby Castle to the War Memorial as part of a Douglas

On a warm spring day in April 2017 horse Charles passes the Villa Marina with tram No. 43 in tow. Once the Promenade refurbishment is completed, the tramway will be on the seaward side of the road at this point. (AUTHOR)

Winter saloon No. 29 is gathering speed along Loch Promenade with horse Charles in charge. This tram is currently away being fully restored. (AUTHOR)

Promenade highway scheme.

The July sitting of Tynwald approved all the recommendations, there was an amendment from the Member for South Douglas that the wording be changed to remove the words 'War Memorial' and insert 'Sea Terminal' to allow this or a future Minister to retain the tramway over its entire length.

Then in a surprise move, the whole application that allowed for a tramway corridor along Loch Promenade, but not actually laying the track, was withdrawn by the Department on 25 July 2016.

On Thursday 11 August Douglas Corporation announced the sale by auction of six 'surplus to requirement' trams, the proceeds going towards the package of support measures to 'assist the Department of Infrastructure in its operation of the tramway'. The sale would be cars 28, 33, 34, 37, 39, and

On 5 August 2017 tram No. 18 was chartered for a wedding special, horse William doing the honours at the front. They are seen here at the Villa Marina waiting for the bride and groom, while tram No. 43 heads towards Derby Castle. (AUTHOR)

ConisterBank
At the heart of the community

FALCON BREWERY
1850

43

WILLIAM

40. The sale date was announced as 27 August, with a viewing day on 16 August.

In a further move that caused some serious concern, Douglas Corporation put the tramway stables up for sale, just a couple of days before the tram auction. The literature for the sale suggested that vacant possession would be early 2017.

The auction duly took place on Saturday 27 August, the total sale value amounting to £9,200, the individual sale prices are shown in the fleet list.

The Island had a general election in September 2016 and as a result a new Chief Minister, who a month or so earlier had purchased on of the six tramcars, and a new Minister for Infrastructure, the department responsible for the Heritage Railways. The new Minister soon made public that he favoured a 'back to basics' plan for the Promenade refurbishment. A few days later the Minister seemed to suggest that leaving the tram lines where they were was still a viable option, a statement that brought a glimmer of hope for the retention of the entire length tramway. In a further

interview with the Minister a few days later, he stated that he wished to keep the tramway on the road and not on the walkway, and that he wanted minimal disruption to the tramway service during the reconstruction of the Promenade. Fancy block paving would be giving way to simpler options.

However, in a remarkable change of heart, the Department announced in December 2016 that it planned to apply for planning permission to reconstruct the Promenades but without the tramway between the War Memorial and Sea Terminal. In an interview soon afterwards, the Minister made the claim

Restoration work nearing completion on Winter saloon No. 27 in the Manx Electric Railway Derby Castle workshops. The superb standard of this work is clearly evident. (AUTHOR)

◄ The final event of the Manx Electric Railway 125 celebrations was a cavalcade of Horse Trams along the Promenade on Sunday 8 September 2018. Here we have tram No. 1 with horse Kewin passing the raised garden in front of the Sefton Hotel. This garden will disappear as part of the refurbishment of the area. (AUTHOR)

▸ Horse William appears to be concentrating more on the photographer than where he is going as he passes the Sefton Hotel with tram 12 in tow on 8 September 2018. (AUTHOR)

▾ Further down the cavalcade were horse Rocky with tram No. 36 and Philip with No. 42, seen passing the Villa Marina. (AUTHOR)

▸ Horse Philip and tram No. 42 pass Greensills corner on Loch Promenade during the return of the cavalcade. 8 September 2018. (AUTHOR)

that there was nothing to be gained by continuing to operate the tramway to its southern terminus. These statements, perhaps not surprisingly, caused uproar among the enthusiast groups and supporters of the tramway.

In various interviews, the Minister attempted to provide positive reasons for suggesting that a truncated tramway would be just as viable as a full length one. Perhaps not surprisingly, the Minister was unable to do so.

Thankfully Tynwald voted to reject the proposal and planned a further debate and vote in January. One of the recently elected MHK's accused the Department of chancing their arm and of insanity, adding that it was ludicrous to terminate the tramway at Broadway both from a heritage value and that it would guarantee a reduction in passenger numbers.

A plan to build temporary stables on part of the former Summerland site,

An impressive line-up consisting of tram Nos. 1, 12, 18, 36, 42, 44 and 45 alongside the Villa Marina. (AUTHOR)

immediately to the north of the Derby Castle terminus, was brought forward by the Department. It was claimed that the existing stables were in need of major repairs and refurbishment.

Various campaigns continued through the new year ahead of the Tynwald sitting on 17 January.

In an amazing sitting of Tynwald, the Department proposals were rejected and an amendment by an East Douglas MHK, to include a single track between the War Memorial and the Sea Terminal, received in favour 17 votes to 14. While the result was welcomed by all concerned with the tramway, there were reservations about the various processes required to get the new plan through planning, given that it would result in a reduction in car parking and that the Promenades are a conservation area.

A week later, the application for permission to build temporary stables on the Summerland site was withdrawn. In February 2017, the Department announced that a 3m wide section of the Loch Promenade either side of the tramway tracks would be resurfaced temporarily. This work was completed before the 2017 season commenced.

Shortly after the commencement of the 2017 season services were suspended

A Festival of Steam was arranged for a week in April 2017, a road train consisting of three traction engines and a low loader conveying Isle of Man Railway locomotive No. 8 Fenella, made a series of journeys on the Island. On the final day of the festival the engines made some trips along the Promenades. Here horse Torrin passes one of the steam engines outside the Gaiety Theatre, with tram No. 45. (AUTHOR)

due to a respiratory infection affecting a number of the horses. At the advice of the tramway vet the horses would be treated and monitored, and it was anticipated that the suspension of services would last around 10 to 14 days. The service resumed on Wednesday 24 May with a restricted service, full services returning on 30 May.

In mid-July, the Department unveiled its latest plans for Douglas Promenade, a £20.7 million scheme to redevelop from Peveril Square to Strathallan Crescent, with work projected to start in September 2018, subject to Tynwald approval.

Thankfully, on Wednesday 19 July, Tynwald in an almost unanimous vote, gave the go ahead for the Promenade works, a project that is expected to take three years to complete. The next stage would be to apply for planning permission.

Douglas Corporation announced in September 2017 that following the failure to sell the tramway stables at an earlier attempt, the buildings would be offered for sale again.

As a result of the planned sale the Department applied again for a smaller, cheaper temporary stable building on the Summerland site. While the previous application had been successful, the cost was deemed too high.

The first of the refurbished trams, Number 36 was in service on the last day of the 2017 season, looking every bit the part, as it made its way along the Promenade.

In January 2018 the Department lodged a planning application for the reconstruction of Loch and Harris Promenades, including the single-track tramway on the seaward side of Loch Promenade. As the northern end of the Promenades are to be reconstructed without any major changes to the position of the tramway or carriageways, there is no requirement for a planning application. The application for the temporary stables was approved in mid-January. The planning department wasted no time on the application for the southern end of the Promenades, approval coming in February, allowing detailed planning to begin on the various construction phases over the projected three-year period.

The 2018 season began on

One of the new Isle of Man Railways tram stop signs, incorporating the new Douglas Bay Horse Tramway logo. (AUTHOR)

Thursday 29 March, the second refurbished tram, Number 45 entering service soon after, followed in very late May by Number 42.

Hardly had the season got underway and plans were announced to demolish the existing tram depot and offices at Strathallan and replace them with a single storey building with a replica frontage. This would provide ground floor office space, secure space for the tramway cars and space for a couple of stored Manx Electric Railway trams. Hot on the heels of this news came the announcement that the Department had negotiated a deal with

Douglas Corporation to purchase the stables for £600,000, considerably less than the original asking price.

Planning consent for the replacement tram shed at Strathallan was received in early July, thus putting in place the final piece of the jigsaw to save this historic tramway for generations to come. The line can now surely look forward to its 150 birthday in 2026 and beyond.

Quite what Thomas Lightfoot would say if he knew his tramway had survived into the 21st century, can only be imagined. He would doubtless be very proud.

Viewed from the Villa Marina, an unidentified horse takes tram No. 45 towards Derby Castle while the Isle of Man Steam Packet vessel *Ben-my-Chree* departs with a sailing to Heysham. (AUTHOR)

STABLES AND TRAMSHEDS

STABLES

When the tramway opened in 1876, the horses were stabled at the private residence of Thomas Lightfoot, known as Athol House, situated near to the current Queens Hotel. It quickly became clear that larger stables would be needed and in 1877 Thomas Lightfoot purchased three terraced houses at the bottom of Burnt Mill Hill (now Summer Hill).

New stables were constructed behind the houses, the stables that are still in use today. Despite being only a few years old, this new facility soon became inadequate and in 1891 it was supplemented by the purchase of No.1 Strathallan Crescent (now occupied by the Kaye Memorial Gardens), which has a sizeable yard and stables and soon became known as 'The Brig'. During World War II the stables at the Brig were used for internees who had misbehaved.

At the very back of the Burnt Mill Hill stables was the Smithy, where the

horses were shoed. In the early years the shoes were handmade from mild steel to suit the various size of horse employed on the tramway. In the month before the season started, the horses were brought in from the fields and the smithy would manufacture around 200 pairs of shoes. Front and back shoes are different, and once made the new shoes would be hung on pegs on the wall beside the forge.

There have been many blacksmiths over the years; more recently, in about 1969, Andy Joughin took over the job, when already in his mid 70s, finally handing over the work to his son, Tom, in 1973. The blacksmiths would have

The current tram sheds are due to be demolished before this book is published. This view inside the shed on 6 August 2016 with car Nos. 1 & 37 shows some of the construction style of the building towards the rear of the shed. (CADE WILLIAMSON)

The Douglas Corporation Horse Box used to transport the horses to their winter pastures, seen at the Stables in May 1989. (AUTHOR)

◄ Remedial work to the trams often took place at the former Cable Tramway depot in York Road, the trams being transferred to and from the Promenade on a small trailer and hauled by a Douglas Corporation Bus. On the eve of the Centenary parade, Royal Tram No. 44 is returning to Derby Castle having been repainted for the occasion. (AUTHOR'S COLLECTION)

▲ A general view of the front of the tram sheds and the offices above, with tram Nos. 21, a Vulcan and No. 1 visible among others during 1964. (AUTHOR'S COLLECTION)

▲ During the early years of the tramway, capturing two double deck cars together would have been commonplace but in more recent times relatively rare. Car Nos 14 and 18 are seen here outside the Derby Castle sheds in May 1990. (AUTHOR'S COLLECTION)

▲ A view of Tramway Terrace and the stables behind. There are two entrances, the bid door straight ahead and the double gate to the far left of the terrace. (AUTHOR)

◄ Resting inside the tram shed are Nos. 12, 36 and 39 during September 2016. This shed is due to be replaced in the coming months. (AUTHOR)

usually had an apprentice working alongside them, that person eventually taking over as the blacksmith and a new apprentice would begin their training. The current blacksmith is Michael Crellin, a long-serving tramway employee. Nowadays, however, ready-made shoes are bought in.

The current stables building has been altered and upgraded over the years; internally the individual stalls have been modified to provide improved conditions for the 24 horses that can be accommodated. A replacement roof was installed over the winter of 1996/97 and in 2009 the chimneys were repaired. The stables yard is a busy place during the season, and still sports its original cobbles, these remaining throughout the older, un-refurbished parts of the building. The horses stabled in the lower loose boxes are brought out into the yard area to have their legs washed, before being led down to the front door, and then a short walk across to the tramway for their stint at the helm of a tram.

The eight lower loose boxes were created in 2004 to replace the fourteen original wooden stalls (seven on each side with a central aisle). Two stalls at the end of the room remain, although they are no longer in use. The whole area is a lot brighter with newly installed lighting, and is a much better environment for the horses to live in. The horses can all see each other over the dividing walls and can also see those opposite them. Each loose box has a tie ring, a large hay rack, automatic drinking bowl, a salt and mineral lick, a manger for feed and wood pellet bedding. The horses are identified by a nameplate hung above each box. Each horse has its own set of harnesses.

The 15 upper loose boxes were created in 2000 to replace the 45 original wooden stalls. The exterior of the building has remained the same. The whole area is very light and spacious, due to the high ceiling, giving a cleaner environment for the horses to live in. Harnesses are stored on pegs along the walkway, and there is also room for large, round bales of hay or haylage.

The feed room is located on the ramp to the upper level and all feed, feed buckets, scoops and various supplements are stored and prepared here. Oats are fed into a hopper above

The workshops of the Manx Electric Railway are refurbishing winter saloon tram No. 27. The two dash panels sit in the workshops with some of the brake handles awaiting refitting to the tram. (AUTHOR)

The final event of Sunday 14 September 2014 was a return trip to the Sea Terminal using double deck tram No. 18. Horse Mark did the honours at the front. With the Mayor and Mayoress on board, Mark pulls away from Derby Castle with a well loaded tram. (AUTHOR)

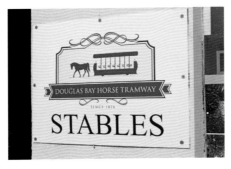

The new Douglas Bay Horse Tramway Stables signage. (AUTHOR)

an oat roller which then crushes them to make them easier to digest, enabling the energy to be quickly obtained.

A new harness room was installed in May 2005. It features a large central table with sink for cleaning harness, and all four walls are lined with hooks for hanging a complete set (collar, hames and bridle). Years ago a saddler was employed to repair the harness, but nowadays they are sent away for any repairs which may be required.

The 'little stable' is a small room off to the side of the yard, containing seven of the original stalls. These stalls are not used now, but have been retained to provide a history of the building. In 2016 it was opened up once more as a small gift shop and exhibition room, containing information and old photos. It can be viewed during the stable tours, which take place throughout the season. During the operational months, the stables are 'home' to the tram horses. Visitors are welcome to look around, either alone or as part of one of the 'Meet the Trammers' guided tours which were introduced with support from the Friends of Douglas Bay Horse Tramway in 2016.

Tramsheds

Initially, when the tramway opened, the three tramcars were stored within the walled garden of Athol House. Following the sale of the tramway to Isle of Man Tramways Ltd in 1882, the new owner built a terminus station and tramcar depot, with accommodation for 12 tramcars, on land opposite Burnt Mill Hill (now Summer Hill) in 1886. In 1891 additional stabling space was gained by the purchase of No.1 Strathallan Crescent, becoming known as The Brig. The yard area allowed a number of tramcars to be stored when not in service. The tramway was sold on again to a new concern, the Douglas & Laxey Coast Electric Tramway

Company in 1894, by when there were 31 trams in the fleet, the majority stored in the open when not in use. The continuing expansion of the fleet to meet growing passenger numbers was the catalyst to the purchase of a plot of land inside the entrance to the Derby Castle Pleasure Grounds in 1895 and a new tram shed was constructed. The new single storey shed had 12 parallel tracks, each long enough for three trams, connected outside by a traverser to avoid a complex pointwork system having to be installed. The building has a cast concrete facade with wooden roller-shutter doors.

A large wooden advert hoarding was erected above the single storey facade and was initially used to promoted the scenic glens served by the electric tramway between Douglas and Ramsey.

When the tramway changed hands again in 1902, being purchased by Douglas Corporation, commercial advertising became abundant, for many years Jacob's Biscuits of one sort or another appeared on the Strathallan Depot hoarding and indeed on the tramcars.

In the early 1900s, and again in the 1920s, internal offices and staff rooms were created within the building, using the space occupied by the far left and right access roads, reducing storage capacity to 30 tramcars. The capacity was further reduced to 27 when, in 1935, the first floor offices were added by Douglas Corporation to house their tramway and bus management staff. The advert hoarding was lost with the addition of the upper floor.

The offices were later used by Isle of Man Transport until 1999 when they moved to a new purpose-built office and bus maintenance facility at Banks Circus. Douglas Corporation then converted the space into the Strathallan Suite, a high-quality conference and meeting suite. A structural survey in 2016 found the building to be life-expired, requiring significant repairs or a complete replacement. In early 2018 a successful planning application will see the existing building demolished and replaced by a single storey shed with a replica facade. Work is expected to start in late 2018, and will provide safe, dry storage for the trams when not in use, along with much needed office space.

On his return to Derby Castle Mark had a word with the dignitaries, to ensure that they did everything possible to save his job and keep the tramway. (AUTHOR)

THE HOME OF REST FOR OLD HORSES

A general view of one of the grazing areas for the horses at the Home. (AUTHOR)

The Home of Rest for Old Horses first came into being in 1950 when sisters Mrs Mildred Royston and Miss May Kermode became dismayed at the number of perfectly fit, but old, working horses being shipped off the Island towards a very doubtful future.

Initially three paddocks and two loose boxes were rented, for 10 shillings (50p) per week, from a retired farrier and his wife, Mr and Mrs Leece, at their property in Abbeylands, just to the north of Douglas. Mrs Violet Leece soon became involved in the project as did Mrs Marjorie Joughin.

One of the first fundraising events was a Christmas fair, held at the Windsor Hotel on Loch Promenade, from where the ladies visited other hotels and public houses, collecting much needed funds. Some gave a farthing, others a whole penny, but it all soon added up to the point where the first pony, Trixie, could be saved. Bess and Sheila soon joined the collection.

During the various collections organised to fund the project, Mrs Royston spoke with a lady who was enthusiastic about the idea and had not realised what fate probably awaited retired working horses from the Island. A few short years later Mrs Royston

The Home of Rest for Old Horses is viewed from Richmond Hill, Douglas in May 2018. (AUTHOR)

received notification of a legacy left by the lady, to allow the purchase of suitable premises for the home. The search was now on.

A suitable old farm, not too far from Douglas, was the ideal and after looking at several properties, Bulrhenny, a 92-acre farm situated on Richmond Hill to the south of Douglas, was purchased in 1955. Huge amounts of work was carried out, removing barbed wire from hedgerows and digging out the stables, and discovering that they had cobbled stone floors. The fields were made secure and soon the horses moved to their new home.

The gift shop started with donations of unwanted gifts from the helpers at the home. Soon another stable was cleared and converted into a café, offering home-baked scones and cakes and of course the always welcome cuppa.

Many volunteers still produce knitted garments for sale in the shop. The home has gradually refurbished further stables and new fencing has been installed as funds permit.

Originally the former tram horses had to be bought from Douglas Corporation, but since 2006 the

Two of the residents pose for the author, who may just have a carrot or two in his pocket. (AUTHOR)

horses just come to the home for a happy retirement.

Since 1950 more than 280 animals have found happy retirement. There are currently around 60 horses and donkeys. They enjoy seeing visitors, in particular those who come with an offering of carrots or apples. Horse feed can be purchased at the home.

A well behaved, that is until food is offered, line up of retired horses at the Home. (AUTHOR)

THE TRAMMERS

Horse William posing for the camera at Derby Castle. (AUTHOR)

The Tramway motive power, the horses are affectionately known as the 'Trammers' and for many are what actually makes the tramway. There are currently around 20 horses in the stud, although this figure is a little fluid at present as new stock is being sought, while others are retired.

Historically, the majority of horses were purchased from Ireland, a mix of cob and farm breeds, old enough to put in harness after brief training and with a working life of perhaps eight years before being sold on to local farms or re-exported.

A mare called Polly, bought from Ireland, had presented Douglas Corporation with a foal named Ramsey

An advert for the 'Meet the Trammers' tours on the side of the stables at Summerhill. (AUTHOR)

in 1966. Due to the significant price rises for good horses in the early 1970s, the Corporation decided to commence its own breeding programme, the first foal being born in 1974. The breeding programme continued through until the 1990s. Mark & Robert were the last in-service 'Trammers' to be bred by the Corporation, Mark retiring during the 2018 season.

Until recently and since the late 1990s, the tramway horses have been purchased locally from the Ballafayle Stud near Ramsey and are either of Clydesdale or Shire breed. A male Clydesdale will typically be 16 to 18 hands (64 to 72 inches, 163 to 182cm) tall and can weight anything up to 2200lbs (1000kg).

In the recent few years new horses have been sourced from either the UK or Ireland and are purchased at around one year old. They are still from the Clydesdale and Shire breeds although some are Cob Cross, a cross between Clydesdale, Shire, Irish Draught and a smaller breed. They spend their first three or so years training in fields with weights, or on the beach with a sledge, before beginning training with a tram. Once fully trained, they work on the Tramway for around 20 years, usually retiring at about 24/25 years old.

On non-operating days they are often taken for a walk in the sea, the salt water being good for their feet and feathers.

They are fed, among other foods, with brewers' grain, a bi-product of the brewing industry and provided locally on the Island by Bushy's Brewery.

Many visitors to the Island enquire about the welfare of the horses. The truth is that they are extremely well looked after, the effort required to pull a fully loaded tram, is only a fraction of that required to plod through a sticky muddy field pulling a plough.During the operating season they only work two, occasionally three return trips in any one day. They spend the winter months grazing in fields around the Island specially reserved for them, with the occasional trip out to show off their power and skills at local ploughing matches. During the season, they also attend the local agricultural shows, one

lucky horse being allowed to show off a full show harness.

Their shoes are generally re-fitted approximately every four weeks, but if a shoe becomes loose it will be changed.

A trip inside the stables and William poses for his picture to be taken. Visitors are welcome at the stables and regular 'Meet the Trammers' tours take place. (AUTHOR)

Keith looks eagerly at the photographer in the hope that there is a stash of carrots or a Polo mint coming his way. (AUTHOR)

OTHER HORSE TRAMWAYS

Historical Horse Tramways

Victor Harbor Tramway (Australia)
Victor Harbor is a coastal town in the City of Victor Harbor, South Australia. The Victor Harbor Horse Drawn Tram links the visitor information centre in downtown Victor Harbor with the nearby Granite Island, home to a wild penguin colony, running for half of its route over a 630m (2,070ft) long viaduct or pier, locally described as a causeway.

It is one of the very few horse-drawn tram routes remaining in public transit service anywhere in the world, and provides service every day throughout the year. There are four tramcars, each hauled by one of eight Clydesdale horses. The line is built to 5ft 3in (1,600mm) broad

Victor Harbor Horse Tramway tram No. 1 departs from Victor Harbor station for its journey across the causeway to Granite Island. (BOB MCKILLOP)

gauge, as were many of the early railways of South Australia.

The South Australian Railways first opened to Victor Harbour in 1864, when a railway pier was constructed. In 1867 the pier was extended to Granite Island, the resulting link becoming known as The Causeway. Railway freight wagons were routinely horse-hauled along this line, but no passenger service was provided until 1894 when the South Australian Railways introduced a new passenger service, utilising an unused horse-drawn tram.

The first tram to be used on The Causeway was a double-ended, double-deck car built in England by 'Brown Marshall' of Birmingham. It had originally been delivered to the Goolwa Railway in 1879, then transferred to the Moonta Horse Railway in 1887, then stored at the South Australian Railways Islington workshop from 1891 until it was sent to Victor Harbor in 1894. Car Number 7 continued in service until 1931.

In 1900 the horse tramway was taken over by private contractors, George and Frank Honeyman, and operated on behalf of the South Australian Railways. By the 1950s The Causeway was in need of repair, but a dispute between the local council and the operators meant that in 1954, when the Causeway was

reconstructed, it was done without the tramway track. The tram service continued operating on Granite Island until 1956, when the service was withdrawn and the trams were disposed of. In December 1956 Keith Roney commenced a tractor-powered, rubber-tyred train service on the reconstructed Causeway. He was succeeded by Jack Edwards and then later by Arnold Stringer who mocked-up a Land Rover to look like a steam engine. This operation continued until the horse-drawn trams were reincarnated in 1986.

The 150th jubilee of South Australia was to be celebrated in 1986, and a special fund was established for projects to mark the jubilee. Reinstatement of the horse tram service was nominated as such a project, and the bid was successful. Replica trams were constructed, the tracks were re-laid and the service recommenced on 14 June 1986.

The tramway, the only Horse Tramway in Australia, is open all year round, one of a few in the world to do so. The line carries around 100,000 passengers annually.

Döbeln Tramway (Germany)
The Döbeln Tramway or Döbelner Straßenbahn is a metre gauge (3ft ⅜in) horse tramway in the German town of

Döbeln. It is the only horse-drawn tramway still operating on its original urban route in Germany.

The Döbeln Tramway was built in 1892 to connect the town' s railway station with its market square. It operated until 1926 when it was replaced by a bus. Throughout this period of operation it remained horse-drawn, and was one of the last horse tramways to remain operational in Germany. After closure, some of its track remained in place and served as a permanent reminder of the old line. Over the years that followed the closure occasional suggestions to restore the line surfaced, but none came to fruition until the beginning of the 21st century.

In 2002 serious flooding in the centre of Döbeln caused considerable damage and significant work was required to restore the town's streets. The opportunity was taken to relay 800m (2,625ft) of track from Obermarkt to Theatre. A former Meißen tram dating from 1899 that had been in use as a hen house for 30 years was acquired and restored as Döbeln Tramway 1. The line re-opened on 9 June 2007.

The line is operated by the Traditionsverein Döbelner Pferdebahn e.V. and is scheduled to operate on the first Saturday of each month from May to October.

Pferde-Eisenbahn, Kerschbaum (Austria)

The first public railway on the European continent opened in 1832, between the Czech Budejovice and Linz Urfahr, and was extended to Gmunden in 1836.

In 1996 a short section of the former Budweis–Linz–Gmunden Horse Railway was re-opened in Rainbach. Half a kilometre of 1.106m (3ft 7.5in) gauge track was re-laid and visitors can now sample the delights of travel by horse-drawn tram.

The luxury tram Hannibal, in which the gentlemen of Habsburg Empire once travelled, operated within the museum that includes the historic Kerschbaum station.

Mrozy–Rudka Tramway (Poland)

In the early 20th century, local workers started to build a sanatorium in the Polish locality of Rudka. In order to get construction materials to the site, a 2km narrow-gauge (900mm) railway was constructed through the forest from Mrozy. Rolling stock was a single wooden wagon hauled by a horse. Once the sanatorium was completed in 1908 the tramway was used to carry convalescents, but still using horses.

The tramway survived through the two world wars until 1967. The line was dismantled in the 1970s, with only some sleepers in high grass remaining as a reminder of the route taken.

However, in 2007 a plan emerged to re-instate the tramway. A copy of the original wagon was manufactured, the track was re-laid and after successful trials in 2011 horse trams returned to the route the following year. The project was awarded the 'National Leader of Innovation & Development – 2012' award.

Ghora Tram (Pakistan)

Ghangha Pur (or Gangapur) is a village in Jaranwala Tehsil in the Faisalabad District of Punjab, Pakistan. It is 193m (636ft) above sea level and part of Union Council 47 of Jaranwala. It has a population of 10,988.

The village has an operational 2ft (610mm) gauge horse-drawn tramway originally built in 1898 to connect it with the Buchiana railway, the station for which is 3km (1.9 miles) south of the village.

The line was originally built to move a large electric motor from Buchania, the motor having arrived there from Lahore by train but there was no easy way to move the motor to Gangapur.

In order to move the motor a special railway track was laid and a horse-hauled trolley was used to bring the motor to the village. It installed a pump to pump water from the canal for agricultural purposes. Once the motor had been moved the line was retained to transport passengers between the two villages.

The tramway remained in service for 100 years when financial issues, and the condition of the track and trolley car, caused it to close in 1998.

Remarkably 12 years later the track was repaired, the trolley rebuilt and the tramway began operating once again on 9 March 2010.

Modern Horse Tramway Rides

Disneyland Paris (France)
Disneyland Park in Paris has horse-drawn streetcars operating on a 3ft (914mm) gauge track, and originally opened in 1992.

Disneyland, California (USA)
Disneyland, Anaheim, California in the United States also has a 3ft (914mm) gauge horse-drawn tramway that originally opened in 1955.

Walt Disney World, Florida (USA)
Walt Disney World, Bay Lake, Florida, United States operated a horse-drawn trolley, again on a 3ft (914mm) gauge track, that opened in 1971.

The Tourist Tramway, Iquique (Chile)
The Chilean capital of Tarapacá region, in the far north of the country, had an operational horsecar system from 1885 through until 1930, surviving an unsuccessful trial with a battery-powered tram in 1917. In the 1920s a number of trams were fitted with gasoline motors, but the system closed altogether in 1930. Seventy years later, in 2000, the city embarked on a project to restore one of its principal thoroughfares, Paseo Baquedano, with wood-planked sidewalks and a horse-powered tramway in the centre. Construction of a metre-gauge line began in 2001 and inauguration finally took place on 24 October 2004.

Koiwai Farm (Japan)
Koiwai is a 3,000-hectare (7,400-acre) private farm situated at the base of Mount Iwate, a volcano that last erupted in 1919 and stands to a height of 2,038m (6,686ft). Koiwai is best known for its dairy products and is a popular tourist destination, with around 750,000 visitors every year.

The farm boasts a large pastoral area known as the Makiba-en, where, among other things, visitors can enjoy a ride on part of the restored 3ft (914mm) gauge horse tramway, originally dating from 1904.

The restored line is a continuous loop, offering views of the farm and upwards to Mount Iwate.

Horse Tram Experiences

National Tramway Museum, Crich (UK)
The National Tramway Museum at Crich in Derbyshire is an Accredited Museum and home to a world-renowned collection of vintage trams. The museum is also home to a vast collection of photographs and archive materials.

The entire collection is designated as being of national importance and the core of the collection is the tramcar fleet which comprises over 80 historic vehicles. The collection contains everything from horse-drawn through to the most advanced all electric vehicles.

Beamish Open Air Museum, Durham (UK)
Beamish, the North of England Open Air Museum, is an open-air museum located near the town of Stanley in County Durham. The museum aims to preserve examples of everyday life in urban and rural North East England from the climax of industrialisation in the early 20th century.

The Beamish Tramway is 1.5 miles long, with four passing loops. The line makes a circuit of the museum site, forming an important element of the visitor transportation system. It is also the longest preserved tramway in the country. It represents the era of electric trams, which were being introduced to meet the growing needs of towns and cities across the North East of England, from the late 1890s, replacing earlier horse-drawn systems that are also included.

Heaton Park Tramway, Manchester (UK) (The Manchester Transport Museum Society)
The Manchester Transport Museum Society Ltd was set up in the early 1960s as the Manchester Transport Historical Collection. The Society aims to preserve documents and artefacts relating to public transport in the Manchester area.

The museum's tramway was opened at Easter 1980 and has operated ever since. The Museum is home to L53, built in the 1880s, and features the Eades Patent reversible truck. Most horse trams were double-ended, requiring the horse to be uncoupled upon reaching the terminus. John Eades' design involved a body that could be rotated on its truck, thus saving time. The tram also only required one staircase, unlike other double-deck trams. This increased seating capacity and reduced the weight.

Timisoara Tramway Museum (Romania)

Established in 2000, Tram Club Banat aims to promote the preservation of the tramways in the Banat. As well as the museum, the group have been involved in the museum services and preservation of the former Arad–Podgoria Electric Railways, the establishing of the tramway museum together with RATT at the Bulevard Take Ionescu depot, and organising historic tram services and private tram tours on the Timisoara system.

The collection currently includes a horse tram built by Waggonfabrik Spearing, Vienna in 1869.

Ballarat Tramway Museum (Australia)

Members of the Ballarat Tramway Museum were aware an odd-looking 'bungalow' behind a house in Ballarat East. On further examination it was identified as a converted horse tram. In 1985 the museum was able to acquire the tramcar and found it to be the original Number 1. Funding to restore the tram was secured within a year, the wheels and parts of an old Melbourne cable tram trailer being utilised for the chassis.

Just over seven years later, after the replacement of several major wooden components including the four main pillars, the resplendent Horse Tram No.1 ventured out onto Wendouree Parade, on 7 November 1992. Horses Ajax and Hercules, two Percheron horses, handled the full loads with great ease.

A special celebration, on 26 December 2012, saw No.1 running through the gardens 125 years to the day since it first entered Wendouree Parade.

Hokkaido Village Museum, Sapporo (Japan)

The Historic Village of Hokkaido is made up of around 60 historic buildings dating from 1868 until 1926 and forms an open air museum. It is located in the Napporo Forest Park suburbs of Sapporo. The museum features four main areas: a town, a fishing village, a farm village and a mountain village.

One of the most popular attractions at the museum is a short double trach horse-drawn tramway that takes visitors along the main street of the village.

The 2ft 6inch (762mm) gauge tramway opened in 1983, and is based on the actual horse-drawn tramline that operated in Sapporo between 1909 and 1918. The line operates from early April to November, and then in the snowy winter months it is replaced by a horse-drawn sleigh.

Ferrymead Heritage Park (New Zealand)

Ferrymead owes its importance in history to the hills dividing Christchurch from the port of Lyttelton. In 1863, the first railway in New Zealand was opened, running from Ferrymead into central Christchurch. This railway line was the inspiration for Ferrymead Heritage Park and the restored railway line follows part of the route today.

It is operated by the Tramway Historical Society, well known for the establishment of the Ferrymead Tramway, an operating tramway at Ferrymead Heritage Park, where restored heritage steam, horse and electric trams recovered from all over South Island can be seen running. The society also operates a small fleet of heritage omnibuses, and a working trolley-bus line with examples of trolley buses from all the trolley bus systems in New Zealand.

Brno Tramway (Czech Republic)

Brno was the third largest city of the former Austro-Hungarian Empire and is today part of the Czech Republic. Brno was the first to open a horse-drawn tram service, which began operating on 17 August 1869. Its route ran to Lažanský-platz (now called Moravské náměstí, or Moravian Square) in the north of the city centre, which was still at the time an independent municipality known as Královo Pole. It was operated by the 'Brno Tramway Society' for transporting both passengers and cargo. The fleet of trams grew from just 6 to 57.

The company, known today as Brno Tramway, was launched in June 1876, with its first route running from the main station (Hauptbahnhof/Hlavní nádraží) to Pisárky. A short while after that a second route was launched. Both routes were operated only during the summer months.

Kazan Tramway (Russia)

In 1875 a horse tramway opened, and later, in 1899, The Kazan Tram system was founded. Six routes operated over 116.20 miles (187km) of track and used a fleet of 197 tramcars. All trams are dark red. The original Kazan tramcar now stands proudly on a plinth, and is in good condition.

Kolkata Tramway (India)

The tram system in the city of Kolkata, West Bengal, India is the only tram network operating in India and is operated by the Calcutta Tramways Company.

The first horse-drawn trams in India ran on the 2.4 mile (3.9km) line between Sealdah and Armenian Ghat Street on 24 February 1873, and discontinued on 20 November of the same year.

Kolkata have run horse trams on special anniversaries in the past but by no means every year.

Berlin Tramway (Germany)

The Berlin Tramway has a collection of heritage trams including an original horse tram which is brought out on special days, such as heritage depot open days.

Stromovka Tramway, Prague (Czech Republic)

The horse tram service commenced on 23 September 1875, along the route Karlín to National Theatre. The line ran approximately along the route of today's Metro Line B. At that time there were several independent suburbs of Prague, now all incorporated into the city. In 1883, the size of the entire network was just over 12 miles (19.43km).

Horse trams still operate on special days.

Danish Tramway Museum, Skjoldenæsholm (Denmark)

Skjoldenæsholm Tramway Museum operated a collection of trams and trains from each of the Danish Railway cities, as well as from other cities around the world. Included in the collection is Horse Tram KSS 51 and the museum offers a ride on a horse tram or horse omnibus on selected days of the season.

Naumburg Tramway (Germany)

A metre-gauge tramway opened on 2 January 1907 and closed due the outbreak of war on 12 April 1945. It however re-opened on 9 December 1945, and closed to passenger service on 30 March 1992.

The line re-opened again on 25 June 1994. The tramway has been continuously enhanced to operate along more and more of the old stretch of 3.36 mile (5.4km) line from Hauptbahnhof to Salztor, via Marientor. The line is operated by museum trams. Preserved horse trams include: Horse tram 133 and Horse tram C 101 dating from 1894.

Spiekerooger Inselbahn (Germany)

The beach on Herrenstrand am Westend was in need of a connection with the nearby village, and on 9 July 1885 a metre-gauge 1.6 kilometre horse tramway opened, operating during the summer bathing months.

The line operated for many years, although truncated in 1932, until after the Second World War when the tram was no longer able to cope with the increased tourism so the horse tramway became the last of its kind to cease operation in Germany in May 1949, the horses being replaced by diesel traction.

In 1981 on Spiekeroog the horse tramway was restored and began operating as part of a museum, the only horse tramway in Germany. A new station building to house the horse train on the station grounds in the village was constructed.

The museum horse-drawn carriage operates several times a day during the summer season, from the station to the Westend. During the winter of 2005/2006 the now worn rails were replaced with redundant rails from the Inselbahn Langeoog. An additional horse was added by the museum in 2017, to allow the horse to be changed daily.

The First day cover issued by Isle of Man Post Office Authority to mark the Centenary of the Tramway in 1976. (AUTHOR)

A Douglas Corporation Horse Tram Bingo card, designed to encourage youngsters to try and see all the horses on the line.

Douglas Bay Tramway Heritage Trust
advancing education through conservation

Douglas Bay Tramway Heritage Trust is a fundraising charity recently established in the Isle of Man to help promote and support the Douglas Bay Horse Tramway, its draught horses and its historic tramcars, with a particular focus on education and heritage conservation.

By providing financial and other assistance, the aims of the Trust are to increase public interest in and knowledge about the Douglas Bay Horse Tramway and the historical use of horses as working animals in transport, industry and agriculture; to help develop and maintain a secure and sustainable future for the Horse Tramway as a heritage transport service and visitor attraction; and to conserve a representative selection of tramcars, equipment, uniform, records, ephemera and other items connected with the Horse Tramway that are of historical and other defined values for sharing with the public.

The Trust's website *www.horsetram.im* provides extensive information about all aspects of the Horse Tramway, current fundraising campaigns and sponsorship schemes, useful contact details, and how to make donations to help with its charitable activities.

DOUGLAS HORSE TRAMWAY CARS FLEETLIST (3'0" Gauge)

No.	Built by	Year	Car Type	No. of seats	Length	Floor Width	Overall Width	Height	Notes
1	Starbuck C&W Co	1876	S/D Saloon	16					Converted to D/Deck 1884/85 Withdrawn about 1900
1	Milnes Voss & Co	1913	S/D Saloon	30	24'8" 7.51m	6'4" 1.94m	6'7" 2.0m	9'11" 3.02m	In service
2	Starbuck C&W Co	1876	Double Deck	36					Broken up 1948/49
3	Starbuck C&W Co	1876	Double Deck	34					Broken up 1948/49
4	Starbuck C&W Co	1882	Double Deck	34					Broken up 1948/49
5	Starbuck C&W Co	1883	Double Deck	34					Broken up 1949
6	Starbuck C&W Co	1883	Double Deck	34					Broken up 1949
7	Starbuck C&W Co	1884	Double Deck	42					Broken up 1924
8	Starbuck C&W Co	1884	Double Deck	42					Broken up 1949
9	Starbuck C&W Co	1885	Toastrack	32	22'9" 6.93m	5'4" 1.62m	6'8" 2.03m	9'6" 2.89m	Broken up 1952
10	Starbuck C&W Co	1885	Toastrack	40	24'0" 7.31m	5'4" 1.62m	6'8" 2.03m	9'6" 2.89m	Broken up 1983
11	Starbuck C&W Co	1886	Toastrack	32	22'9" 6.93m	5'4" 1.62m	6'8" 2.03m	9'6" 2.89m	Stored Jurby Transport Museum
12	Milnes	1888	Toastrack	32	22'9" 6.93m	5'4" 1.62m	6'8" 2.03m	9'6" 2.89m	In service
13	MRCW Saltley	1883	Double Deck	42	22'6" 6.85m	6'0" 1.82m	10'8" 3.25m		From South Shields 1887 Renumbered 14 in 1908 [1]
14	MRCW Saltley	1883	Double Deck	42	22'6" 6.85m	6'0" 1.82m	10'8" 3.25m		From South Shields 1887 Destroyed by rock fall at the depot in 1908
15	MRCW Saltley	1883	Double Deck	42	22'6" 6.85m	6'0" 1.82m	10'8" 3.25m		From South Shields 1887 Last used 1939. Broken up 1949
16	MRCW Saltley	1883	Double Deck	42	22'6" 6.85m	6'0" 1.82m	10'8" 3.25m		From South Shields 1887 Broken up 1915
17	MRCW Saltley	1883	Double Deck	42	22'6" 6.85m	6'0" 1.82m	10'8" 3.25m		From South Shields 1887 Converted to S/Deck 1903 Broken up 1917

18	MRCW Saltley	1883	Double Deck	42	23'1" 7.03m	6'1" 1.85m	6'4" 1.93m	10'8" 3.25m	From South Shields 1887 Converted to S/Deck in 1903–6, Back to D/Deck 1988/9. In service
19	Milnes	1889	Toastrack	32	22'9" 6.93m	5'4" 1.62m	6'8" 2.03m	9'6" 2.89m	Withdrawn 1949 Broken up 1952
20	Milnes	1889	Toastrack	32	22'9" 6.93m	5'4" 1.62m	6'8" 2.03m	9'6" 2.89m	Withdrawn 1949 Broken up 1952
21	Milnes	1890	Toastrack	40	24'8" 7.51m	5'4" 1.62m	6'11" 2.09m		In service
22	Milnes	1890	Toastrack	32	22'5" 6.83m	5'5" 1.65m	6'10" 2.08m	9'9" 2.79m	Withdrawn 1978. On Display at Jurby Transport Museum
23	Milnes	1891	Toastrack	32	22'8" 6.90m	5'5" 1.65m	6'11" 2.10m		Broken up 1952
24	Milnes	1891	Toastrack	32	22'8" 6.90m	5'5" 1.65m	6'11" 2.10m		Broken up 1952
25	Milnes	1891	Toastrack	32	22'8" 6.90m	5'5" 1.65m	6'11" 2.10m		Broken up 1952
26	Milnes	1891	Toastrack	32	22'8" 6.90m	5'5" 1.65m	6'11" 2.10m		Broken up 1974
27	Milnes	1892	Winter saloon	30	24'5" 7.44m	5'10" 1.77m	6'6" 1.98m	9'2" 2.79m	In service [2]
28	Milnes	1892	Winter saloon	30	24'5" 7.44m	5'10" 1.77m	6'6" 1.98m	9'2" 2.79m	Sold 27/8/2016 for £2,800
29	Milnes	1892	Winter saloon	30	24'5" 7.44m	5'10" 1.77m	6'6" 1.98m	9'2" 2.79m	In service [2]
30	Milnes	1894	Toastrack	32	22'6" 6.85m	5'5" 1.65m	6'10" 2.08m		Broken up 1952
31	Milnes	1894	Toastrack	32	22'6" 6.85m	5'5" 1.65m	6'10" 2.08m		Broken up 1987
32	Milnes	1896	Toastrack	32	21'8" 6.60m	5'4" 1.62m	6'10" 2.08m	8'7" 2.61m	In service
33	Milnes	1896	Toastrack	32	21'8" 6.60m	5'4" 1.62m	6'10" 2.08m	8'7" 2.61m	Sold 27/8/2016 for £1,200
34	Milnes	1896	Toastrack	32	21'8" 6.60m	5'4" 1.62m	6'10" 2.08m	8'7" 2.61m	Sold 27/8/2016 for £1,300

35	Milnes	1896	Toastrack	32	21'8" 6.60m	5'4" 1.62m	6'10" 2.08m	8'7" 2.61m	In service
36	Milnes	1896	Toastrack	40	24'11" 7.59m	5'4" 1.62m	6'10" 2.08m	8'7" 2.61m	In service
37	Milnes	1896	Toastrack	32	21'8" 6.60m	5'4' 1.62m	6'10" 2.08m	8'7" 2.61m	Sold 27/8/2016 for £1,100
38	Milnes	1902	Toastrack	40	24'5" 7.44m	5'5" 1.65m	6'11" 2.10m	8'7" 2.61m	In service
39	Milnes	1902	Toastrack	40	23'0" 7.01m	5'5" 1.65m	6'11" 2.10m	8'9" 2.67m	Sold 27/8/2016 for £1,800
40	Milnes	1902	Toastrack	40	24'5" 7.44m	5'4" 1.62m	6'10" 2.08m	8'11" 2.72m	Sold 27/8/2016 for £1,000
41	Milnes Voss & Co	1905	Toastrack	32	23'3" 7.08m	5'6" 1.67m	7'1" 2.16m		Renumbered 10 in 1985, Withdrawn 1988 and broken up
42	Milnes Voss & Co	1905	Toastrack	40	24'8" 7.51m	5'5" 1.65m	7'0" 2.13m	9'1" 2.77m	In service
43	United Electric Car Company	1907	Toastrack	40	24'6" 7.46m	5'5" 1.65m	6'11" 2.10m	8'10" 2.69m	In service
44	United Electric Car Company	1907	Toastrack	40	24'6" 7.46m	5'5" 1.65m	6'11" 2.10m	8'10" 2.69m	In service [3]
45	Milnes Voss & Co	1908	Toastrack	40	25'0" 7.62m	5'6" 1.67m	7'0" 2.13m	8'6" 2.59m	In service
46	Milnes Voss & Co	1909	Toastrack	40	24'11" 7.59m	5'5" 1.65m	6'11" 2.10m	8'11" 2.71m	Withdrawn 1987 Displayed at Woodside Ferry Terminal from 1990 until broken up in 2001.
47	Milnes Voss & Co	1911	Toastrack	40	25'1" 7.64m	5'5" 1.65m	7'0" 2.13m	8'9" 2.66m	Withdrawn 1978 Stored Jurby Transport Museum.
48	Vulcan Motor	1935	Saloon/ Toastrack/ Convertible	27/34	25'6" 7.77m	5'7" 1.70m	6'11" 2.10m	8'6" 2.59m	Withdrawn 1980 Broken up 1982
49	Vulcan Motor	1935	Saloon/ Toastrack/ Convertible	27/34	25'6" 7.77m	5'7" 1.70m	6'11" 2.10m	8'6" 2.59m	Withdrawn 1980 [4] Stored Ramsey

50	Vulcan Motor	1935	Saloon/ Toastrack/ Convertible	27/34 7.77m	25'6" 1.70m	5'7" 2.10m	6'11" 2.59m	8'6" Withdrawn 1980 Broken up 1982

Notes:

[1] Left the Island in 1955, later displayed at the Museum of British Transport, Clapham, returning for the centenary celebrations of 1976 and now on display in the Manx Museum, Douglas.

[2] Originally built without platform vestibules, which were added in 1895.

[3] The Royal car, having been used on several occasions to convey members of the royal family.

[4] Property of the Isle of Man Railway and Tramway Preservation Society, currently stored in Ramsey.

Tram No. 45 dating from 1908 has a peek out of the open 'People' door of the tram sheds on 20 December 2011.
(AUTHOR)

About the Author

Barry Edwards was born and brought up in South West London. His interest in railways stems from his father who spent his entire working life with British Railways. Barry made his first visit to the Isle of Man in 1976, by chance coinciding with the centenary of the Douglas Horse Tramway.

An interest in photography, and in 1981 the acquisition of a Mamiya 645 medium format film camera, soon led to the first published photograph, a class 31 diesel locomotive at London Paddington station. For many years all black and white film processing and printing was done in a home-built darkroom.

The visits to the Island became ever more frequent and the collection of monochrome negatives grew, eventually leading to the first book *The Railways and Tramways of the Isle of Man* in 1993, published to mark the centenary of the Manx Electric Railway. This was followed by further titles, and then, in 1998, the probably inevitable move to the Island.

Being resident allowed a more extensive coverage of the railways, initially with the film camera. A second-hand digital camera was purchased in 2006, the digital age eventually embraced with the purchase of a Nikon DSLR in 2008.

This new book covering the history of the Douglas Bay Horse Tramway is his 18th book, the 6th for Lily Publications; these have included titles about the railways, the various airlines that have served the Island and the story of the Peel Cars.

Bibliography

Isle of Man Tramways, F K Pearson, David & Charles, 1970, ISBN 0-7153-4740-3

Railways and Tramways of the Isle of Man, Barry Edwards, OPC, 1993, ISBN 0-86093-507-8

Isle of Man Railways Locomotive, Tram and Rolling Stock Directory, Barry Edwards, B&C Publications, 1996, ISBN 0-9527756-3-8

The Douglas Horse Tramway, Keith Pearson, Adam Gordon, 1999, ISBN 1-874422-25-7

Trams of the Isle of Man, Stan Basnett, Lily Publications, 2009, ISBN 978-1-899602-19-3

Manx Transport Fleet List 2015, Barry Edwards, Blackboards Publishing, 2015, ISBN 978-0-9932474-0-8

Horse Trams of the British Isles, R W Rush, Oakwood Press, 2004, ISBN 978-0-8536-1600-9

Travellers Companion; The Douglas Bay Horse Tramway, Grant Taylor, Isle of Man Railways, 2016, No ISBN.

The Manx Transport Systems, William Lambden, The Omnibus Society, 1965, No ISBN.

Trains & Trams of the Isle of Man, Barry Edwards, Lily Publications, 2010 & 2014, ISBN 978-1-907945-93-9